Coping with China

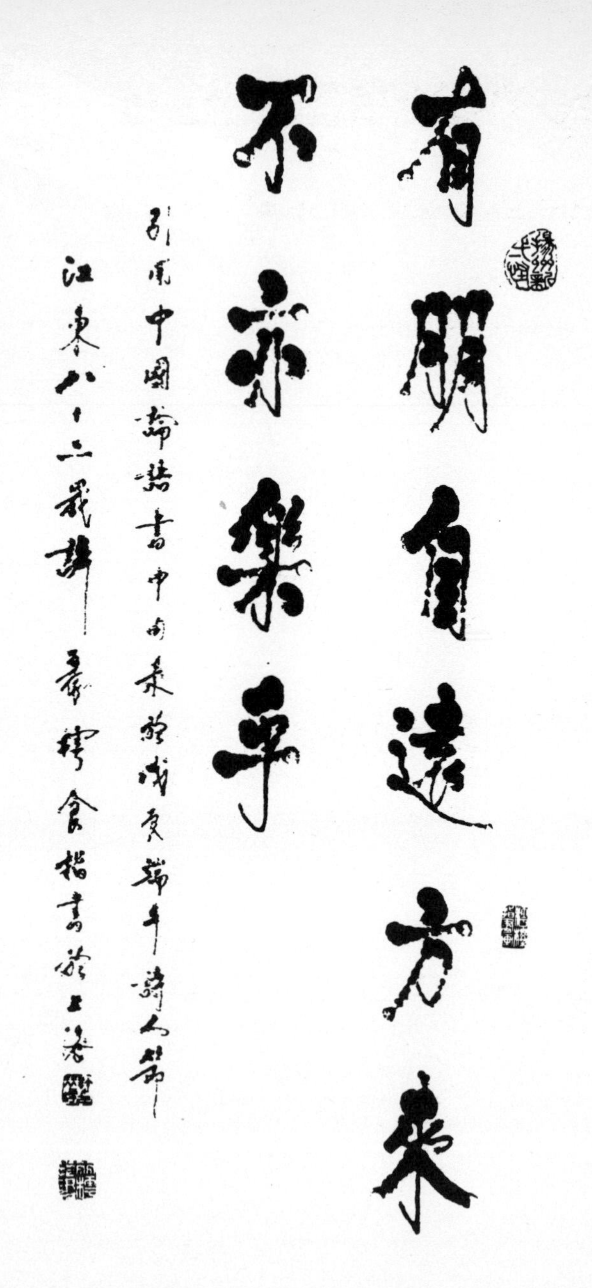

'Is it not a glorious thing when friends come from afar?' Confucius (551–479 BC).
Finger-calligraphy by Xu Lichu

Coping with China

Richard King and Sandra Schatzky

Basil Blackwell

Copyright ©Richard King and Sandra Schatzky 1991

First published 1991

Basil Blackwell Ltd
108 Cowley Road, Oxford, OX4 1JF, UK

Basil Blackwell Inc.
3 Cambridge Center
Cambridge, Massachusetts 02142, USA

All rights reserved. Except for the quotation of short passages for the purposes of criticism and review, no part of this publication may be reproduced, stored in a retrieval system, or transmitted, in any form or by any means, electronic, mechanical, photocopying, recording or otherwise, without the prior permission of the publisher.

Except in the United States of America, this book is sold subject to the condition that it shall not, by way of trade or otherwise, be lent, re-sold, hired out, or otherwise circulated without the publisher's prior consent in any form of binding or cover other than that in which it is published and without a similar condition including this condition being imposed on the subsequent purchaser.

British Library Cataloguing in Publication Data

A CIP catalogue record for this book is available from the British Library.

Library of Congress Cataloging in Publication Data
King, Richard.
Coping with China/Richard King and Sandra Schatzky.
p. cm.
Bibliography: p.
Includes index.
ISBN 0-631-16213-5 ISBN 0-631-16214-3 (pbk.)
1. China – Description and travel – 1976- – Guide-books.
I. Schatzky, Sandra. II. Title.
DS705.K48 1989
915.1′ 0458 – dc19

Typeset in 10 on 11½ pt Sabon
by Dobbie Typesetting Limited
Printed in Great Britain by Billing and Sons Ltd, Worcester

Contents

Acknowledgements

The cartoons on pp. 13 and 63 are reproduced by kind permission of *Punch*

The cartoon on p. 2 is reproduced from the *Victoria Times-Colonist* by kind permission of Adrian Raeside

The cartoon by Eugene Theroux on p. 135 is reproduced by kind permission of the *China Business Review*

'Spoiling the view' is reproduced from *Chinese Satire and Humour: Selected Cartoons of Hua Junwu (1955–1982)*, translated by W. H. F. Jenner, with the translator's permission

'Corruption' is reproduced by kind permission of Morgan Chua and the *Far Eastern Economic Review*

'Peace' and 'Home' by Tan Huay Peng, taken from *Fun with Chinese Characters, vol. 1*, are reproduced courtesy of Federal Publications (S) Pte Ltd

'The Answer' is reproduced from *The August Sleepwalker*, by Bei Dao, translated by Bonnie S. McDougall, Anvil Press Poetry (London, 1988)

The extract from *The Book of Songs* is reproduced by kind permission of Cyril Birch from his *Anthology of Chinese Literature*, Penguin (Harmondsworth, 1967)

The authors wish to thank also the following past and present residents of China for their suggestions and advice: Alison Bailey, Ed and Margaret Berry, Colleen Davidson, Bennett Lee, Lorraine Lewis, Ramona Mar, Beth McKillop, Sandra Sachs and Barry Till. Thanks also to Cindy Bailey, Stella Chan, Ralph Huenemann and Kathlyn Liscomb.

Introduction

When the tanks of the People's Liberation Army rumbled into Tiananmen Square in the early hours of 4 June 1989, they destroyed more than the encampment of students who had occupied the heart of Beijing for the previous fifty days. By killing hundreds of demonstrators and bystanders, China's leaders and their army effectively destroyed the legitimacy of their claim to represent and defend the people they rule. Deng Xiaoping, China's most powerful leader throughout the 1980s, had seemed assured of a place in history for the economic reforms and political pragmatism which rescued the nation from stagnation and dogmatism and brought China back into the international community. In the early 1990s, as the Deng era draws to a close, he will be remembered first and foremost as the man who sent in troops to massacre civilians as the world watched in horror.

Outrage overseas was combined with alarm at the potential for instability in China. Foreign businesspeople, students and other residents left China as soon as they could, and contracts and loans then being negotiated were put on hold or abandoned. Most Chinese students overseas chose to stay where they were rather than return to repression at home. Tourism had earned China over $2 thousand million in 1988, and there had been predictions that earnings would rise to five times that amount by the end of the century. Instead, the tourist industry slumped, and newly-built hotels were left almost empty.

Yet in the short term at least, it appears that China's leaders have managed to restore a measure of stability to the country, and thereby avoided being swept away by the tide of democratic reform that pushed through Eastern Europe in 1989. A year after the Tiananmen massacres, there are signs that the Chinese government is succeeding in its attempts to normalize relations with the rest of the world. Though the leadership warns the Chinese people constantly about the evils of Western ideas, it has also made it clear that economic reform, which depends on foreign technology and capital, will continue. Foreign businesspeople have returned to China, led by the Japanese, with overseas Chinese, Europeans and North Americans following them. The US administration chose to renew China's most favoured nation trading status, a privilege it continues to deny the Soviet Union, thus encouraging American companies to continue to conduct business with China. Tourism is also recovering; the number of visitors in 1990 is approaching 1988 levels, with visitors from Taiwan making up much of the shortfall from fewer Western tourists.

However, the stability that China's leaders have managed to impose is fragile. There is widespread discontent at the government's handling of the economy, coupled with anger at the suppression of protest. The freedoms briefly tasted in the spring of 1989 are proving harder than ever for China's leaders to deny.

'Tiananmen Square Flower' by Adrian Raeside

As foreigners return to China, they will find themselves alternately enchanted and frustrated, as visitors to China have been for centuries. With the much needed foreign currency they carry, they will also, perhaps unwittingly, take with them styles, tastes and attitudes to which many young Chinese people aspire, and which the Chinese leadership opposes. For some Chinese, the allure of the outside world is tinged with resentment of the wealth of the visitors. They remember past indignities China suffered at the hands of foreign powers, and are angry at the preferential treatment that foreigners are still accorded by Chinese authorities today. While some people may view foreigners as the means to get rich, Chinese officials frequently regard them as demanding and tiresome nuisances.

Yet, however many people visit their country, the Chinese, formally at least, still regard the relationship between themselves and foreigners as that of host and guest. The Chinese host is honour bound to provide for the guest. In turn, the visitor has an obligation to be courteous—the Chinese word for politeness means literally 'the manners of a guest'. Foreigners in China are assigned to host organizations, which are responsible both to the guest, for making suitable arrangements, and to the authorities, for assuring the welfare of the foreign guests and accounting for their eccentricities and misdemeanors.

Visitors to China find themselves regarded not so much as individuals but as representatives of their country. Some people find this role uncomfortable or even galling, but it is inevitable that it will happen, and visitors do well to accept it with good grace and a heightened awareness of the possible impact of their words and actions. Equally unavoidable is the fact that Westerners will find themselves objects of considerable curiosity, even when they are doing the simplest or most personal things. This is a feature of being foreign in China that some visitors find flattering, and they miss the attention when they return home. Others react with irritation, anger or alarm. A sense of humour is an asset in dealing with the crowds that may gather.

Being in China as a foreigner, maddening as it might sometimes be, is always an intense and memorable experience. This book is an attempt to ease the process of coping with an ancient society as it lurches towards the twenty-first century. We have not written a guide-book in the traditional sense. Other, longer, books (listed in the further reading section at the end of the book) can be consulted for details of the collection at Beijing's Historical Museum, the natural wonders of Guilin and Jiuzhaigou, the best stores in Shanghai or the best beaches on Hainan Island. Instead, we have prepared an introduction to the cultural traditions and administrative complexities that have made outsiders view China as both fascinating and inscrutable.

Perhaps the best spirit in which to approach China is that of the bamboo so admired by generations of Chinese scholars and artists. Bamboo is gentle and relaxed when the climate is favorable, flexible enough to bend under strong winds, yet sufficiently resilient to spring back from adversity and stand tall again. These are qualities which will serve foreigners well, as they deal with the kindness and the suspicion, the generosity and the officiousness that they will encounter in China.

And if you wish to know more (as the writers of China's classic novels told their audiences), you must read the chapters that follow.

Getting there

Visas

Visas are issued by Chinese embassies and consulates. In Hong Kong you can get them at China International Travel Service (CITS). Processing an application by mail can take up to two months, but is considerably faster in person. CITS in Hong Kong can often complete the process the same day. (See Useful addresses.) Visas can also be obtained at points of entry into China, such as international airports, as long as all documentation is complete.

Application procedure

Visa application forms can be obtained from the Chinese embassy or consulate nearest you. Alternatively, they can be picked up from travel agents and tour companies handling China tours.

The visa application form requires you to provide basic personal information, dates of your visit to China, and the places you intend to visit. People planning to visit relatives or friends are required to provide names and addresses of those they will be visiting. Visa application forms should be filled out in duplicate, and sent or taken with two photographs and a passport to a Chinese embassy or consulate. There is a visa application fee of £6.40, $11 US, $13 CDN or the equivalent in the country of application. (Amounts of money are at Spring 1990 levels unless otherwise stated.)

Types of visa

Visas are issued to reflect the purpose of your visit – diplomacy, business, visiting relatives, study, teaching or tourism. The type of visa you have will directly influence the range of things you can do in China, how much they will cost you, and even whether or not you will be able to purchase certain consumer goods.

Be sure to apply for the appropriate type of visa.

Tourist Members of tour-groups should send their completed application forms and passports to their tour organizer, who arranges for all members of the group to be included on a group visa. If you are planning to stay in China to travel longer than your group does, you should arrange to have an individual tourist visa instead of being included with the group.

Business Businesspeople travelling to China must have a formal letter of invitation from an organization authorized to invite foreigners to China. The letter should accompany your visa application. If you have no contact already, the commercial attaché at a Chinese embassy or consulate can make recommendations.

Students and teachers Students applying for a student visa will need to include a letter of acceptance from a Chinese university with their visa application forms. Teachers should include a letter of invitation from the institution at which they will be teaching. In the case of academics invited to lecture in China, the host institution is generally responsible for securing authorization for a visa.

Children People who travel with children and include children's names on the passport of one parent should consider getting each child his or her own passport and visa. Occasionally people have found that if they have a child's name on their visa and have to make an unexpected trip outside the country without the child, there can be delays while the situation is explained and a lecture delivered on making sure the child is with you next time. Alternatively, if the other parent wishes to travel outside China with the child, it can be more cumbersome to arrange travel documents.

Medicals Students and teachers who plan to be at Chinese institutions for an academic year or more must have a medical examination before a visa can be issued. A medical form can be obtained with your visa application form. It must be completed by a doctor, following a complete medical examination which includes a chest X-ray and an AIDS test. Take the X-ray as well as the report on it, otherwise you run the risk of being subjected to a fluoroscope examination, which results in higher exposure to radiation than X-ray machines in use in the West. You may also want to take disposable syringes in case university authorities insist on taking blood to repeat the AIDS test, as has occasionally happened.

Applying to teach

Many Chinese universities and colleges and even some secondary schools are keen to recruit native speakers of English to teach in their institutions. Qualifications in teaching English as a second language are respected, as are higher degrees (MA, Ph.D.). Inquiries should be directed to the education officer at the Chinese embassy or consulate nearest your home. These education officers can supply you with a list of institutions which hire foreign teachers. Write directly to institutions at which you would like to work. Be prepared to apply to many places to succeed at one. Alternatively, you can seek a placement through the State Bureau of Foreign Experts; write to the Bureau directly at PO Box 300, Beijing.

The best way of finding a job in China, as with most other arrangements Chinese, is through a personal introduction or connection. If you are introduced to a Chinese institution by one of the several thousand Chinese students and academics studying in the West, your chances of a favourable reply (or any reply at all) are greater. Ask your contact for a letter of introduction to send with your application.

The wheels will turn slowly with respect to your inquiries and you will not be kept up to date with developments concerning your application. When an invitation to teach is finally issued, it may come only a few days before the start of term. The reason behind this could be that the institution in China has only just secured permission or funding to hire you, or that another candidate has cancelled an application at the last moment. This sort of delay makes it difficult for those with families or job commitments at home to contemplate teaching in China. Keep in mind that if you are offered a position too late to be able to make arrangements, you may be able to negotiate a year's deferral in your appointment. For information on categories of teachers and working conditions, see Settling in.

Study in China

Many Western countries have government-sponsored student scholarships which send a limited number of students, usually China specialists, to China for one or two years. For information regarding these programmes, in the UK, contact: The British Council, 10 Spring Gardens, London SW1A 2BN. In Canada, contact the Chinese Embassy in Ottawa. In Australia: Department of Employment, Education and Training, PO Box 826, ACT, 2606. In the US: Committee on Scholarly Communications with the PRC, National Academy of Sciences, 2101 Constitution Avenue NW, Washington DC 20418.

An increasing number of Western universities which offer degree programmes in Chinese or Asian Studies have arrangements with Chinese 'sister' institutions where students can spend all or part of an academic year in the Chinese institution and have their studies accredited towards their degree. These programmes are open only to registered students of those universities.

Several American schools have established programmes in China which are not restricted to their own students. Two of the better established are: Wellesley College-CET in Beijing (CET, 1110 Washington Street, Boston, MA 02124) and the Duke Study in China Program in Beijing and Nanjing (Duke University, 2111 Campus Drive, Durham, NC 27706). The Council for International Educational Exchange (205 E. 42nd Street, New York, NY 10017) is a federation of American schools which arranges for study at a number of centres in China. Fees for these programmes are at least US$2500 per semester for classes and accommodation.

A cheaper option (up to US$1500 per semester and $1.50 a day for accommodation) is to contact a Chinese university that accepts foreign students (a list of these universities and courses offered can be obtained from Chinese embassy or consulate education officers). A word of caution: standards of teaching are higher in internationally-monitored programmes, and credits for their courses are more likely to be recognized by Western universities.

Getting to China

By air

Flying is still the most popular way for most people to get to China. However, international air service to China on nonChinese carriers has not yet returned to Spring 1989 levels, a reflection of the sharp decline in group travel since June of that year. Pricing information becomes outdated quickly and is affected by promotions and seasonal fluctuations. This information is best obtained from a travel agent or directly from an airline. A travel agent can save you the trouble of calling around for the best fare and routing. Discount fares are easiest to find in London (where the market is deregulated). Substantially better deals than the airlines offer on flights to Hong Kong can often be found through Chinatown travel agencies.

When buying tickets, book any connecting domestic flights you may need within China at the same time. These arrangements are considerably easier to make outside China than inside. It will be necessary for you to reconfirm onward flights once you are in China. This can be done through CITS or the Chinese national airline CAAC (Civilian Aviation Administration of China or its affiliates). While it is theoretically possible to reconfirm flights by telephone, it is generally more effective to do so in person.

Travellers should be aware that luggage allowances on internal Chinese flights are not as generous as international allowances. One piece of carry-on and 20 kilos (44 lbs) of checked luggage is what is permitted, and while a group's bags are seldom weighed, an individual's may be. Excess baggage charges are one per cent of the ticket price per excess kilo.

Air China, the international arm of CAAC (not to be confused with the Taiwanese carrier China

Airlines), has flights connecting Beijing with New York, San Francisco, Vancouver, Sydney, London and several continental European cities. Air China is not the most service-oriented of airlines, and it is as well to know the alternatives.

Major routes

From eastern US Travellers have the option of flying over the Atlantic or the Pacific. Either way it will be necessary to have a stopover or make connecting flights. Various options are possible if the Atlantic route is selected (see below). For the trans-Pacific route, onward flights can be taken from the west coast. An alternative is a direct New York–Tokyo flight, offered by Japan Air Lines (JAL) or United, with a connection following a night's rest at Tokyo's Narita Airport. Connections are by Air China to Beijing, or the CAAC affiliate China Eastern to Shanghai.

From US west coast There are direct flights to Beijing from Los Angeles. The Tokyo stopover option is also available from JAL for travellers from San Francisco and Seattle. The San Francisco–Hong Kong route is served by the Hong Kong airline Cathay Pacific, Korean and Singapore Airlines.

From Canada Flights for Hong Kong and Tokyo depart Vancouver. (Canadian Airlines' service to Beijing and Shanghai is currently suspended.) Canadian and JAL serve Tokyo; Canadian, Cathay Pacific and other carriers serve Hong Kong.

From UK and Europe British Airways flies to Beijing and Hong Kong from Heathrow. It also flies to Hong Kong from Manchester. A number of other carriers fly from Heathrow to Hong Kong. Continental European cities with direct air routes to China include Paris, Geneva, Frankfurt and Helsinki.

From Australasia Qantas has flights to Hong Kong from Sydney and Perth. Cathay Pacific flies from Melbourne and Auckland to Hong Kong. Air New Zealand flies from Auckland to Hong Kong.

From Hong Kong Air China flies from Hong Kong to a number of Chinese cities; some destinations in

South China (including Shanghai) are also served by the largely Chinese-owned Dragonair. Hong Kong–Beijing and Hong Kong–Shanghai flights are often fully booked weeks ahead, but a number of standby tickets are usually available. The most common destination from Hong Kong is Guangzhou, with three flights daily from Kai Tak Airport. Other options for Guangzhou include: a hovercraft, a hydrofoil, a ferry, an express train or the combination of local train to the Chinese border, a walk over a wooden bridge and another train to Guangzhou. (This last option is for the romantically inclined; it takes ages and does not save you much.) Ferries and cruise ships to Shanghai, Xiamen and other southern port cities are another way to get into China from Hong Kong. The CITS office in Hong Kong can handle arrangements for any of these options.

Overland

For those who enjoy train travel and have lots of time, the Trans-Siberian Express, which runs from Moscow to Beijing, is a wonderful way to get to China. Each week there are two trains leaving Moscow, one staffed by Chinese personnel, the other by Soviet. You can choose to travel in one of three classes: hard compartment, soft compartment (both accommodating four, with toilets at the end of the car) or deluxe (accommodating two, and sharing toilet with one other compartment). The Chinese train goes via Ulan Bator in Mongolia and takes five days. The Soviet train travels to Beijing via Manchuria and takes a day longer. We recommend the Chinese train, but whichever option you choose, you should go prepared with plenty of reading material, toilet paper and lots of snacks. A Russian phrase-book is useful for communicating with the staff of the dining car.

For travellers who like something even more out of the ordinary, there are overland routes from Kathmandu in Nepal to Tibet and from Islamabad in Pakistan to Kashgar in Xinjiang on China's western frontier. Hunt around for tour operators who will guide you (at considerable expense) on these routes. Solo travel by local transportation is possible but should be undertaken only by the extremely robust and intrepid.

Touring

Solo travel

China has been admitting individual travellers since 1978. For those who do not like group travel or being hurried onto tour buses, this may be the way to go.

However, travellers making their own arrangements should expect the mechanics of travel to take a very high proportion of their time. China's transportation system is overloaded, and a wait of a week for a seat on a train is not unusual. Much of the headache of making travel arrangements can be saved by asking CITS in Hong Kong to design a personalized Foreign Independent Tourist (FIT) package tour, which will include transportation, hotel reservations, transfers from airports and railway stations to hotels, and guide-interpreters. Air and rail fares and hotel rooms work out to be about twice as costly booked individually as they would be in a group tour.

Solo travel is becoming increasingly popular with backpackers, who like to head away from the popular tourist spots and explore the less foreigner-frequented parts of China. Backpackers can travel cheaply on local buses or by bicycle, and stay at inexpensive hostels, but they must be prepared to deal with people who speak no English and who may make no efforts to assist them with travel arrangements. We have heard of one unfortunate foreigner who waited a week for a train which never arrived, while down the street she could have caught one of several daily buses to her destination. Problems can sometimes be overcome with a rudimentary knowledge of Chinese and a backpacker's guidebook.

Group travel Group travel has been the option preferred by the majority of visitors to China. At the time of writing, group travel from the West is nowhere near the record levels of 1988, but a partial recovery seems likely. Though the solo traveller claims to see more of the 'real China', the group traveller certainly sees more of the sights in much less time, and in much greater comfort. A large number of companies offer tours at a wide range of prices and some tours include other Asian countries. Pick up all the brochures you can find, and as you leaf through them, consider carefully.

Itinerary What do you want to see? If you only plan on going to China once (beware: the place can get under your skin!), you should certainly visit the capital Beijing and the nearby Great Wall, and Shanghai, China's largest and most exciting city. Most tours include these two,

"'Ow do! I'm the Duke of Edinburgh and this is . . ."

Reproduced by courtesy of *Punch*

plus Guangzhou and two or three other cities. An interest in archaeology may take you to Xi'an, ancient capital and site of major tomb excavations. For natural scenery, you might choose to go to the spectacular karst formations of Guilin, which have inspired artists for generations, or Mount Emei in Sichuan. Hangzhou is the place for artificial scenery, and for gardens you should visit Suzhou. All of these are regular stops on the tourist routes and well worth a visit, but no tour will take you to them all.

Some tours follow a theme, like the Silk Road tours, which take the overland routes of medieval trade caravans through China's north-west to Pakistan. Tours of 'Classical China' include the ancient capitals of Xi'an, Luoyang and Kaifeng. Others head into the minority or non-Han Chinese areas of Mongolia, Xinjiang and, most exotic of all, Tibet. Prices are higher the further you go inland, and a greater proportion of time is spent on buses and trains or in airports. The more out-of-the-way destinations are perhaps better saved for a second or third trip.

Special interest Those who want to pursue specific interests, such as hiking, cycling, motorbikes, botany, martial arts and meditation, may have to look a little further than the local travel agent, but should persevere!

Universities, art galleries and other special interest groups can design their own itineraries with CITS. These groups often arrange to stay in Chinese colleges to save on costs. For help in finding tours of this kind, check at universities with departments of Asian or Chinese studies, and with museums and art galleries in your area.

Friendship tours Volunteer organizations promoting friendship with and understanding of China offer reasonably-priced tours, sometimes involving fairly spartan accommodation. On their study tours particularly, there is an attempt to provide more background information than might be found on a standard commercial tour. Friendship organizations also hold periodic meetings about China, and can provide information for prospective travellers. (See Useful addresses.)

Tour organizers What can the tour company offer? Tour operators buy tour packages from CITS, which arranges transportation, accommodation and activities within China. CITS also provides English-speaking guides at every stop along the way. The quality of service you get from CITS on a budget tour is about the same as on higher-priced tours, but by paying more you ensure that, where available, you stay in modern, international-class and foreign-managed hotels rather than older buildings with more exciting plumbing.

No brochure can fully prepare you for the beauties and delights that await the traveller to China—or for the frustrating delays at the airport while the flight-crew has its siesta, and the late-night arrivals at darkened train stations with no waiting bus. (These are merely minor disasters, which make good stories to tell your friends when you get home, and should not be allowed to spoil your holiday.)

Tour leaders

The tour operator supplies a tour leader or guide whose skill and experience (or lack thereof) can make a big difference to your holiday. A tour leader who understands China's history, culture, social system and language is an enormous asset, not only in explaining the background to what you are seeing, but also in pre-empting and dealing with difficulties (especially important as some Chinese guides tend to evaporate in contentious and embarrassing situations).

Customs regulations

When you enter China, you will be required to list valuables, especially electronic goods such as cameras, calculators and video- and audio-cassettes, which you will have to take out with you when you leave. You can take in pretty much anything (barring pornography, habit-forming drugs, radio transmitters, firearms and political or religious propaganda) as long as you take it out again. Keep your customs declaration and report if something listed on it is stolen or lost. Thefts should be reported to the Public Security Bureau (PSB – the police), and a note from the PSB documenting your report should be saved for customs.

Customs officers generally take a very relaxed attitude to tourists. They are more rigorous with longer-term visitors like students and teachers, especially on re-entries after trips home or to Hong Kong. Avoid promising to buy too much for Chinese friends. Customs regulations are most strictly enforced for overseas Chinese, who are permitted to take in one 'large piece' of equipment (such as VCR, TV, fridge) and two 'small pieces' (such as radio, watch, sewing-machine) duty-free to give to relatives, but must pay heavy duty for additional items. Adults may take in 400 cigarettes and two litres of alcoholic liquor.

Insurance

Do not go to China without adequate coverage. Should there be a medical emergency, you must have insurance that will fly you home if necessary. Take the phone number of your insurance company or agent with you.

Things to take The variety and supply of goods in Chinese stores and markets is constantly improving, thanks to the economic liberalization of the 1980s. It is unnecessary to take many daily-use items.

Pharmaceutical The exceptions are pharmaceutical goods like prescription drugs, familiar medications, contraceptives and first-aid supplies. Sunscreen and mosquito repellant can be useful. Some people prefer to take along disposable syringes so that if they require injections, they need not be concerned about whether or not syringes have been adequately sterilized. Sanitary napkins and tampons may not be available in some cities.

Mechanical Those who will be living in China for an extended period of time may find that having a cassette-player and tapes of favourite music offers the escape and relaxation needed to prepare them for the next challenge. Coverage of international events in the Chinese English-language media is steadily improving; however, a short-wave radio to pick up BBC, Radio Canada International and Voice of America broadcasts is still useful for keeping in touch.

Other useful paraphernalia might include an electric razor and a hair-dryer. The current in China is 220 volts. North Americans with 110-volt equipment should either take an adaptor, use batteries or buy new. Wall outlets are not standardized. They come in a range of two- and three-pin varieties, which include round two-pin 'shaving plugs', flat two-pin plugs like standard North American issue and international standard three-pin plugs. Adaptors are usually available at Friendship Stores and hotels. Chinese batteries are not particularly long-lasting (one brand has the unfortunate and appropriate name of White Elephant). You may want to take rechargeable batteries and a recharger that works on a 220-volt current.

Clothing Despite some rather daring fashions in Shanghai and Guangzhou, most of China is conservative in its dress. Revealing clothing worn by Western women is unsuitable, since it will attract attention and reinforce unfavourable stereotypes. For winter, take long thermal underwear, woollens, thick socks and waterproof shoes, even if you will be in the south. South of the Yangtze River, the Chinese do not heat buildings in winter, or do so for a couple of hours a day at most, even when the temperatures dip below freezing. They respond to cold by adding more layers of clothing. This is effective, but some Westerners find the extra bulk required to stay warm uncomfortable.

Other useful items to take include a glue-stick for sealing envelopes and marker-pens for writing addresses on parcels to be mailed.

Attitude

A spirit of adventure and a determination to relish the unexpected may be the most useful thing you can take to China. Things seldom go as they might be expected to, and the unpredictable experiences can be the most rewarding if taken in the right spirit.

Settling in

First impressions

Crowds

Chinese cities are very densely populated, and homes are small, so Chinese citizens spend more of their time out on the street than their Western counterparts. The crush of humanity on busy shopping streets like Beijing's Wangfujing and Shanghai's Nanjing Road can be off-putting for those used to a quiet life. To make matters worse, stopping to stare at foreigners can slow things down still further. Stares may be blank, but they are not hostile, and a simple greeting will often raise a smile. If you find yourself drawing a crowd, do not stand too long or play to the audience, either of which might bring the street to a standstill.

Two major groups of Chinese people seek out foreigners on the street: students wanting to practise their English and black-market money-changers. The first group can be interesting and helpful companions if their grasp of English permits conversation. The second should be ignored and avoided – not only is what they are doing illegal, they also have many tricks for short-changing the unwary.

Public hygiene

If you are at all squeamish or have a poor sense of balance, use hotel washrooms wherever possible and avoid public toilets other than those set aside for foreigners at tourist sites. Municipal authorities in the capital, concerned for the reputation of their city, have begun to construct luxurious pay-as-you-use public washrooms, and have instituted a monthly 'top toilet' contest. Other cities are distinctly less well provided with sanitary public facilities. Further afield, Chinese toilets generally feature rows of holes to squat over, sometimes with dividers between them, but rarely with doors—leading some to joke about China's 'open-door' policy. Toilet paper and running water are by no means universally available, so it is a good idea to carry paper and moist towelettes with you.

Toilets in restaurants are a better bet. They generally have doors, and are as often sit-down as squat, but standards of cleanliness vary. Relief may be at hand – the Beijing Tourism Administration has a vigilante squad of toilet inspectors making spot-checks on restaurants, with the power to close down unsanitary premises. It is to be hoped that other cities follow suit.

Spitting

Public spitting is a common, noisy and unsanitary practice. Efforts have been made in recent years to curb indiscriminate spitting, and spittoons with lids are provided in many public places. Authorities in some tourist cities have designated 'culture streets' where, in deference to foreign sensitivities, spitting is prohibited. However, if you hear the sound of hawking from the person walking or cycling ahead of you, be prepared to take evasive action.

A roof over your head

There is a wide range of accommodation available for travellers, with an appropriate range of prices, particularly in the major centres where most foreigners visit and work.

Top of the line

Hotels that are members of international chains have all been put up in the hotel-building boom that started in 1980. Many of them were completed just as tourism collapsed in June 1989. Low rates of occupancy have induced some hotels to discount their rates substantially; reduced rates can often be obtained during the winter months. Most of the new foreign-managed hotels can be booked by a travel agent (or yourself) before you leave for China. Rates are generally quoted in US dollars. Full price rooms generally exceed $100 for a double room, or considerably more for Japanese-run hotels. A partial list of the more established international hotels includes:

In Beijing: Holiday Inn Lido, Great Wall Sheraton, Shangri-la, Jianguo Hotel, Hotel Beijing-Toronto.
In Shanghai: Huating Sheraton, Nikko Longbai, Shanghai Hilton, Holiday Inn.

In Guangzhou: China Hotel (New World International), Garden Hotel (Peninsula/Swissôtel), Holiday Inn.

In Tianjin: Crystal Palace (Swissôtel), Holiday Inn.

In Xi'an: Golden Flower (Trust House Forte) and Garden Hotel (Mitsui), Holiday Inn, Jianguo Hotel Xi'an.

Alternatives Other hotels can be booked through CITS. It is generally possible to book in one city for another. CITS charges a fee for making the reservation, and can also arrange for you to be met at a station or airport and taken to the hotel. Alternatively, you can just go to a hotel and take a chance on its having space. Most do outside the April–October tourist season, but there is no guarantee of accommodation. You have to go in person if you want to negotiate a student rate. Many hotel managers will refuse to admit to having a student discount at first but will relent if business is slack and the student is insistent and civil. A student card is not always demanded.

Prices for Chinese-run hotels vary enormously depending on city and standard of accommodation, the most expensive being in the range of the international hotels, the cheapest a tenth of it. Hotels dating from the colonial period of the 1930s and 40s, like Shanghai's Peace Park and Shanghai Mansions, may not be as well-equipped and luxurious as the international hotels, but they can be stylish and gracious in their way, and are more centrally located. Hotels built to Russian designs in the 1950s and 60s are showing their age. Even hotels put up in the 1970s are in varying states of repair. Visitors with official connections may be able to stay at guest houses operated by various ministries and bureaux for high-level official guests. Many of these are now being opened to foreign guests as a means of acquiring foreign exchange.

Travellers' complaints about substandard service, dirty rooms and poor food in Chinese hotels (Guilin is a main offender in this respect) have, after considerable delay, been noted by CITS and the hotel industry. These complaints, combined with the competition engendered by the proliferation of hotels and the example set by the international chains, have led to more attention being paid to the expectations of foreign hotel guests. Training programmes for hotel staff have been introduced, and pay scales have been restructured to reward improved performance.

Bottom of the line

At the lowest end of the accommodation market, the shoestring traveller can find dormitory accommodation in many towns, either through guidebooks or by looking out for the entrepreneurs who hang around bus- and rail-stations and offer cheap rooms to Chinese travellers. Other solo travellers are a good source of information. With cheap accommodation, expect what you pay for. Further afield, temples sometimes offer lodging to travellers visiting religious sites.

Residence permits

All foreigners living in China for extended periods of time must register with the PSB and be issued a residence permit. Arrangements for this should be made through the host institution, or by going to the local PSB office.

The student life

Third-world countries have been sending students to Chinese technical universities and medical schools since the 1950s, and in the early 1970s and 80s China signed bilateral student exchange agreements with many Western countries. Numbers of foreign students in China have mushroomed since the normalization of relations between China and the United States in 1979.

Funds for higher education are tight in China, and students from overseas are a major source of revenue and foreign exchange. Chinese universities make considerable efforts to attract Western students by signing agreements with foreign universities and by advertising programmes for individual students.

Foreign students at most Chinese universities stay in specially built foreign student dormitories and have meals, classes and other activities as a group, apart from Chinese students on the same campus. Rooms are adequate but not luxurious (bare floors, beds, desks, chairs, overhead fluorescent lighting, minimal or no curtains), and are usually shared with one other person. Students from Japan tend to take as many as possible of the conveniences of home (television, VCR, microwave etc.), but life is possible without them. Elsewhere on campus, the Chinese students are six or eight to a similar-sized room. Bathroom and cooking facilities are communal, and there is generally hot water for showers for only an hour or two each day. Foreign student dormitories are an international community, and fascinating exchanges or petty misunderstandings can result as different cultures interact. There is little there in the way of Chinese culture, though; for that, foreign students must make contact with Chinese students or explore Chinese society beyond the campus gates.

The Chinese authorities categorize foreign students as either *zifei*, 'paying for themselves', or *gongfei*, 'publicly funded'. This second group includes government exchange students and those who are in China on reciprocal agreements with Western universities. *Zifei* students pay fees and board; *gongfei* students do not pay for tuition and lodging and are given a monthly allowance currently set at 283 *yuan* to cover food and some travel. In addition, while *zifei* students travel at resident foreigner rates, *gongfei* students are given a 'white card' which entitles them, in theory at least, to pay Chinese prices and use Chinese money (*Renminbi*) in place of Foreign Exchange Certificates (see Money).

(The 'white cards' are now, confusingly, orange, though they are still referred to by their former colour. Rumours persist that they will be phased out, but it has not happened yet.)

Instruction for foreign students is not generally the main attraction of study at a Chinese university. The real education is to be had outside the classroom in the opportunity to observe and participate in Chinese society.

The 'Expert' life

Foreigners working for Chinese institutions are usually called 'experts'. They are either housed in hotels and bussed to and from work or, increasingly as hotel prices rise to levels that Chinese institutions cannot afford, housed where they work. This latter option, though less comfortable than hotel life, nevertheless has the advantage of integrating the 'expert' into the life of the institution. Accommodation is typically of the small and austere kind supplied to Chinese colleagues, though sometimes concessions are made, such as superior food, some heating (in the south) or more heating (in the north). 'Experts' are issued with a 'privilege card' that corresponds to a *gongfei* student's 'white card'.

'Experts' are paid differently from place to place, but scales of pay are generally geared to educational qualifications. At the top end, academics with a Ph.D. degree regularly earn over 1000 *yuan* a month, a princely sum by Chinese standards. This is paid either in a combination of standard Chinese currency (RMB) and Foreign Exchange Certificates, or exclusively in RMB. At the low end of the scale, English language teachers with no more than a BA degree may be classified as 'foreign teachers' (as opposed to 'experts'); pay is around 300 *yuan*, which allows for comfortable survival but not much more.

Before setting off for China, the prospective 'expert' should find out what courses he or she will be teaching and what materials are available. Library and photocopying facilities tend to be limited, and it helps to take more than one copy of required readings.

Chinese students are enthusiastic and highly motivated. Great demands are placed on foreign teachers to provide extra tutoring and conversation, which can result in 'expert' burnout. It is advisable to specify office hours rather than undertaking to be available all the time.

The journalist life

Journalists are only grudgingly tolerated by the Chinese authorities. Their motives are suspected, and their contacts and activities are monitored. The range of information considered to be classified is far greater than in a Western country, which means that reading between the lines of official pronouncements is often the only way to find what is really happening in the corridors of power. Foreign journalists and film-crews may be sought out by dissidents and demonstrators as a way of getting a message to the outside world, but this is an exercise fraught with danger for the Chinese informants.

The Chinese press is tightly controlled by the authorities, and generally publishes only officially sanctioned news. After relative liberalization through most of the 1980s, more rigid controls were in place as the decade ended. Communist Party General Secretary Jiang Zemin defined the role of the press in China as 'accurately and vividly reflecting the Party's political standpoint, principles and policies.'

Spousework The Chinese government does not allow husbands and wives of diplomatic personnel to work outside their embassies. There is, however, often work to be found by the spouses of businesspeople and 'experts'. Such work is more likely to be interesting than high paying. Business offices of foreign companies frequently employ expatriate spouses (and moonlighting foreign students) in secretarial, assistant and research positions, for which the going rate is about 15–30 *yuan* per hour. 'Expert' spouses are usually in demand where they are, either as teachers of English or in positions tailored to their expertise, though they are often paid at less than the 'expert' rate.

Childcare Representatives of foreign companies who want to hire an *ayi* (nanny), must do so from the state-owned Foreign Enterprise Service Corporation (FESCO). Diplomatic personnel must go to the Diplomatic Service Bureau of the Foreign Ministry. Both organizations charge high rates, only a small part of which is passed on to the *ayi* herself. Arrangements for securing an *ayi* can sometimes take a long time. Be sure to inquire whether or not you will have the right to change *ayi*s if for some reason there are problems. 'Experts' with children should make arrangements through their employers. Westerners involved in Joint Ventures (see Business) can bypass FESCO and arrange childcare through their Chinese partners.

Schools Foreign residents in China can put their children into the Chinese school system. While many parents may feel that these children will benefit from the experience, others may prefer an English-language education in an international setting. The International School of Beijing at the Lido Centre on Jichang Road teaches a Western curriculum to students aged 5–15 (from grade 1 to grade 9 and plans to introduce a full high school curriculum). Fees are US$6250 per annum at 1990 rates. There is a smaller and rather more expensive international school in Shanghai.

Laundry

Modern hotels have laundry and dry-cleaning services that are efficient and no more expensive than at major hotels in other countries. Guests at older hotels have occasionally found that clothes have come back in a smaller size than when sent out. For this reason, we recommend you leave clothing which requires particular care at home. In older hotels, the laundry process may take longer if the weather is wet. Most Chinese universities have a laundry service for students which is very reasonable. People who prefer to do their own laundry can buy Chinese laundry soap in powder or bar form. It is amazing how much you can wash in a small hand-basin!

Post and telephone

Internal postage rates have remained constant since the 1950s: letters and cards are 4 *fen* (Chinese cents) in the same city and 8 *fen* outside; airmail letters within China are ten 10 *fen*. The domestic mail service is extremely efficient, with city deliveries made twice a day. It is often faster to write to someone to make arrangements for meeting than it is to try to get through by phone. International airmail rates rise steadily; at the time of writing the rate for a letter is 2.00 *yuan*, 1.60 *yuan* for a postcard.

Stamps can be purchased, and letters sent, from hotels, nearly all of which handle mail, or from post offices. Letters can be mailed at post-boxes, which are painted green. Chinese envelopes are not pre-glued, but pots of glue are generally available. (These can be messy, hence the hint about the glue-stick in the previous chapter.)

Parcels can be sent from many hotels and main post offices. Outside hotels, it is common practice to show what you are sending to post office officials before you wrap it up. Take your own tape, string and brown paper, or a piece of cloth, needle and thread if you want to follow Chinese custom and sew small items into cloth packages. Marker-pens are useful for labelling these packages, and are not yet generally available.

At local post offices you can send telegrams within China and buy registered money orders. For both of these services you need to be able to write Chinese.

Public pay-phones are a rarity in China, but shops, university dormitories and some public buildings have phones which can often be used for local calls, sometimes for a small charge. Hotel rooms have telephones. There is no charge for local calls, though it can take a while to get an outside line, as demand on the limited circuits is considerable. Overseas calls can be direct-dialled from international hotels and offices or apartment buildings; elsewhere, calls must be booked through the operator, and can take some time to complete. The whole of China runs on Beijing time; daylight savings time runs from mid-April to mid-September. When the time is 12 noon in China, it is 8 p.m. the previous day in San Francisco and Vancouver, 11 p.m. in New York and Toronto, 4 a.m. in London and 2 p.m. in Melbourne.

The Chinese authorities monitor telephone calls and mail. Perhaps because of this, incoming mail often takes much longer to arrive than outgoing. However, mail usually arrives undamaged except for clumsy repacking of the occasional parcel, or over-generous application of glue sticking a letter to its envelope.

Fax Fax machines can be found at most international hotels, particularly those with business centres.

Getting around

The mechanics of travel can take a long time. It is not uncommon for Chinese people to spend all day getting plane or train tickets, a process which can involve hours spent in queues, pleading for favours or judicious gift-giving. Though CITS, Foreign Exchange Certificates and a foreign face can sometimes speed things along, acquiring tickets is still a much slower business than in the West.

Air

Air-travel within China has until recently been the monopoly of CAAC. Two developments signal the beginning of the end of that monopoly. CAAC has decentralized its domestic business by creating six regional subsidiaries, though the parent company still retains overall control of routes and pricing. Perhaps more significantly, the Air Force of the People's Liberation Army (PLA) has established a rival airline, Lianhe (United), to compete with CAAC on some routes. Lianhe is still a small airline with limited equipment and routing, using military rather than civilian airfields, but one can hope that the competition will improve air travel service and safety in China.

CAAC

CAAC is with good reason one of the most maligned airlines in the world. Safety regulations are sloppily enforced: seat belts are often in disrepair; passengers are allowed to take on too much hand baggage, which is then piled in the aisles; and extra passengers are sometimes squeezed on. Crews are in short supply and fly more hours than most international carriers would permit. This may account for the punctilious adherence to after-lunch siestas, even if flights are scheduled and passengers waiting.

Many of the planes used on domestic flights are Russian jets dating from the Sino-Soviet alliance of the

1950s, or Chinese copies of them. CAAC still flies turbo-props of even earlier vintage – one British tourist in the early 1980s remarked that he had flown missions in the Second World War in a plane like the one we were on. Maintaining such a diverse fleet is a technical nightmare, and standards of maintenance are not high.

CAAC is conscious of its poor reputation. It is working to improve its fleet, its performance and its image. Boeing planes assembled in China are destined for service with CAAC, and other new acquisitions are planned. CAAC's expansion and upgrading is on a scale never before attempted by a national civilian airline (though shortage of foreign exchange and trained staff may slow the modernization process).

Tickets Airline tickets can be bought at CAAC offices and major hotels in the city of departure. Although CAAC has a computerized reservation system, it is not usually possible to book connecting or returning flights. Travel agents in Hong Kong can make reservations for onward flights, but the passenger is still required to confirm the flight for each departure, a process which can be as time-consuming and frustrating as buying the ticket. CAAC reservations agents are characteristically inefficient and rude, and have been known to ignore all reservations and resell tickets to first-comers when the computers are down. Planes often fail to leave on schedule, delays are seldom announced, even in Chinese, and CAAC does not take responsibility for passengers inconvenienced by delays (though foreign passengers are sometimes fed and found hotel rooms, if delays are overnight). There are no refunds for missed flights.

Fares CAAC charges higher fares to foreign visitors and businesspeople than to Chinese customers, foreign students and employees of Chinese institutions. For example, a one-way Beijing–Shanghai flight which (at spring 1990 prices) cost 377 *yuan* for the highest-paying group would be 264 *yuan* for students and 'experts.' In addition, holders of 'white cards' can save by paying in RMB. Prices for Chinese travellers, which used to be less than half of the lower rate, have risen sharply in recent months in response to a significant growth in domestic travel among the entrepreneurial *nouveau riche*.

Rail

Train travel is slower than air, but more efficient, safer and cheaper. An additional appeal for devotees of railways is that many of China's locomotives are steam-powered, especially in the coal-rich north. China only recently ceased production of steam locomotives. The Chinese rail system has 50,000 kilometres (31,000 miles) of track, links all major cities except Lhasa, and serves over a thousand million travellers a year with remarkably few delays and inconveniences. Express trains linking major cities travel at an average speed of 65 kilometres (40 miles) an hour. Local trains, and some long-distance services, stop frequently and are very slow.

Classes

Apart from the express trains which take passengers from Hong Kong or the border station at Shenzhen to Guangzhou and which are uniformly luxurious, most trains within China have three classes.

Soft class serves tourists and other foreign travellers, Party officials, army officers and, increasingly, the new entrepreneurial class. Compartments have four berths, comfortable seats with antimacassars, soft beds with sheets, and a washroom at each end of every carriage. Meals are served for soft class passengers in the train's dining-car. Since these meals are generally expensive and heavy, many travellers prefer to take instant noodles and fruit for some of their meals. Soft class passengers also have the luxury of sitting in comfortable waiting rooms in stations while the masses throng the platforms.

Hard sleeper carriages have bunks stacked three high, six to an open compartment, and are, as their name suggests, hard. There are toilets and sinks at each end of the carriage. At mealtimes passengers buy a coupon which they exchange for a hot meal in a square tin (or, on some routes, a polystyrene box, which the attendants throw out of the windows after the meal) from a trolley wheeled through the carriage.

Hard sleeper carriages are always crowded, and there is no restriction on smoking, which can make the air very unpleasant on long journeys. Still, they are some of the most relaxed and informal places for conversation in the country. CITS always tries to book foreigners into soft class, but students and 'experts' travel regularly in hard sleepers at a saving of almost half the soft class fare.

Hard seat, the cheapest way to ride, is fine for short trips, but only for the hard-up and masochistic on journeys of any length. Carriages are absolutely packed. There are passengers standing or squatting in corridors and at the feet of those lucky enough to have reserved or fought for a seat. Gaining admittance to the carriage's single toilet can require both a trek of epic proportions and a strong stomach.

Travellers in hard sleeper and hard seat carriages should go prepared with their own snacks, toilet paper, hand-towel and mug for tea-drinking and tooth-brushing (something that should only be done with boiled water).

Fares Foreign travellers pay about double the Chinese price for soft class on the trains, a sum which is reduced by about 30 per cent for resident foreigners. *Gongfei* students and 'experts' with the white cards can buy rail-tickets at Chinese prices. Some foreign travellers try to avoid higher prices by asking Chinese friends to buy tickets for them. Railway officials are on to the practice and will impose the surcharge if they find this has happened.

Boats Chinese steamers service a number of routes along the China coast and major inland waterways. Chinese ships have five classes, ranging from the presidential, through comfortable shared cabins (the usual foreign tourist class), to medium and large dormitories and steerage class in the bowels of the boat. The luxury cruise liners that ply the coast have varying rates depending on the location of cabins.

A popular inland voyage is through the spectacular gorges of the Yangtze River. Shorter boat-rides arranged by CITS for tourists include: the six-hour ride from Guilin to Yangshuo along the Li River, through what must surely be China's most photographed scenery; along sections of the Grand Canal, built in the seventh century to take tribute grain from the south to northern capitals; and on scenic lakes like Hangzhou's West Lake and Wuxi's Lake Tai. The boat-trip from Shanghai to the mouth of the Yangtze, which can be taken on a CITS launch or a Chinese tourist boat, is delightful on a clear day and tedious on a foggy one.

Coaches and buses

Not all of the over 250 cities and regions open to tourists are on the rail network. In some areas, long-distance coaches are run by CITS and can be booked through them. The coaches are smooth-running and air-conditioned, with reserved seating and a video-player at the front showing martial-arts movies day and night. Out of the tourist areas, stand in line with the masses for tickets on bouncy old buses ventilated by open windows, onto which passengers are allowed until it is jammed full. A seat is a distinct advantage on a long and bumpy road. To make the trip more diverting, be warned that on downhill stretches drivers will cut the engine and coast to save fuel, that passengers in rural areas are allowed to bring their livestock with them and that travel sickness is common among Chinese passengers.

On long coach and bus journeys there are periodic brief stops for food and the call of nature. Speed is recommended – drivers do not wait when it is time to leave!

Within cities

Beijing has a modern subway system, consisting of an east–west commuter line and a central loop which serves several places of interest to the visitor (the railway station, the Friendship Store and the zoo). Tickets to go anywhere cost 30 Chinese cents.

For other parts of Beijing, and for all other cities, the alternative is the commonest form of public transport – local buses. English-language street-maps of major cities have bus routes which are clear and easy to follow once you have worked out which way you are pointing. Fares are reasonable, ranging from 10 to 40

Chinese cents. There are no transfers and no return tickets, so you buy a ticket for each bus you ride. The conductress sits in the rear portion of the bus. Tell her where you want to go (or show a piece of paper with the place-name written on it) and give her a small bill. Your ticket and change will be passed back. When not selling tickets, the conductress can sometimes be observed leaning out of the window to batter the side of the bus with the handle of a small flag and scream at cyclists to get out of the way.

Chinese buses are very crowded. Try to avoid using them at rush-hours. Also be sure to hold on to your wallet or purse; pickpockets have resurfaced in China and often work on buses.

Taxis Taxis can be found at hotels, which often have special taxi offices, and at tourist spots. They can also be ordered by telephone. In Guangzhou taxis cruise and can be hailed. (To hail a cab, stand at the kerb with hand extended at waist level and wave; pointing and waving with the hand held high are considered rude.) Fares are 1.20 *yuan* per kilometre, 1.80 for a one-way trip beyond inner-city limits. Minimum charge is 6.80. Drivers should give receipts. If there is a dispute over the fare, make note of the driver's licence number and the details of the trip, and report the problem to the authorities.

Some drivers are unwilling to make long trips out of town if it is likely they will have to return empty. If you are planning to return after a short while, it is often easier to pay the driver waiting time than it is to find another taxi when you want one.

Private taxis, a relatively new form of Chinese free enterprise, have no meters and drivers will charge whatever they think the market can stand. For foreign passengers this is often well above the going rate. Either stick with registered taxis with meters, or negotiate the price before getting in, then pay that amount. Private taxi-drivers' reputation for civility and honest service is about on a par with that of cabbies in New York City.

Cars and drivers can be hired by the day from CITS (subject to availability) for around 100 *yuan*, which is good value when split between two or three people. It is far quicker than the buses when you plan to do a lot of sightseeing.

Bicycles

Bicycles, the preferred form of transport for most Chinese people, should be bought by anyone intending to stay any length of time. A basic black one-speed sells for around 200 *yuan*, travels well on bumpy roads and has good resale value. Bicycles must be registered with city authorities. In some cities, it is possible to purchase bike insurance. Make enquiries, since petty theft is on the rise in China. Bicycles can often be rented by the day from bicycle repair shops.

Cycling in China seems perilous at first. Other cyclists do not signal much, there are no lights on bicycles, and trucks and cars come very close. Still, most people adapt fairly quickly. Wider roads sometimes have cycle-paths on the extreme right, and these should be used, even though they make left turns even more hazardous. Cycling is forbidden on some busy shopping streets. Dismount and push your bicycle until the no-cycling section ends. In the suburbs, many Chinese ride pillion on the luggage rack behind the seat. This is rather hard on the rear tyre, the pedaller's legs and the passenger's bottom. Traffic police in towns may instruct the passenger to get off or even impose a fine.

Cars

Getting a car is a straightforward process, but takes time and money. The car would need to be heavily used over a long period to make the purchase worthwhile. Volkswagen Santanas assembled in Shanghai and AMC Jeeps assembled in Beijing can be ordered in China. A cheaper alternative for Beijing residents is to order a Toyota from the company's representative in the Noble Tower office complex and have it shipped from Japan to Tianjin, where it can be picked up and cleared through customs. In Guangdong province, cars can be ordered from Hong Kong dealers.

Customs duties for cars brought in by foreign companies can be very high (over 250 per cent in some instances). Diplomats are exempted from customs duty. Chinese–foreign Joint Ventures are supposed to get preferential treatment from customs, though this is not always the case in practice. Driver's licences are handled by municipal authorities and rules for getting them vary. Usually a valid driving licence from another country can be exchanged for a Chinese licence without the test the authorities have a right to impose.

Foreign drivers should take care to be amply insured since in the event of an accident they may be held at least partially responsible even if they were not at fault.

Money

The Chinese government maintains control of the nation's money supply, and forbids the exporting or importing of its currency. Chinese currency can be obtained at points of entry, hotels catering to foreigners, Friendship Stores and banks at a rate of exchange set by the Bank of China. The rate for traveller's cheques is slightly higher than that paid on cash.

The unit of currency is the *yuan*. As of June 1990, £1 buys 7.91 *yuan*, $1 US buys 4.71 *yuan*, $1 CDN buys 4.00 and $1 AUS buys 3.61 *yuan*. At these rates, 1 *yuan* is worth 12.5 pence, 21 cents US, 25 cents CDN and 27 cents AUS.

The *yuan* declined against most currencies during the 1980s, as the rapid growth in the Chinese economy gave rise to inflation significantly higher than in the industrialized nations. (For example, the *yuan* lost half of its value against the US dollar between 1981 and 1986.) By the end of the decade, inflation was officially estimated at over 20%, with food costs leading the way. Prices of goods, services, transportation and especially accommodation for foreigners have also risen sharply in recent years. During most of the 1980s, the Bank of China seemed content to let the *yuan* slide to increase export potential, but has recently moved to limit the money supply to combat inflation.

A *yuan* is referred to colloquially as a *kuai*. It divides into 10 *jiao* (colloquial term: *mao*), each of which in turn divides into 10 *fen* or cents. There are 100 *fen* in a *yuan*. An English-speaking sales assistant might refer to the sum of 1.25 *yuan* as 'one *yuan* and twenty-five *fen*' or 'one *yuan* and twenty-five cents'; in Chinese he or she would call the same amount 'one *kuai* two *mao* five'.

1 *yuan* in *Renminbi* (People's currency)

BANK OF CHINA
FOREIGN EXCHANGE CERTIFICATE

本券的元与人民币元等值。
本券只限在中国境内指定的范围使用。不得挂失。

The yuan expressed in this certificate is equivalent in value to the Renminbi yuan.
This certificate can only be used within China at designated places. No request to register its loss will be accepted by the Bank.

ONE YUAN

1

1 *yuan* in Foreign Exchange Certificates

Dual-currency system

China operates what is effectively a two-currency system. One currency, designed for use by foreigners, is called Foreign Exchange Certificates (FECs). The other is the regular 'people's currency' *Renminbi* (RMB).

FECs

Foreign money and traveller's cheques are changed into FECs, which are called *waihui* in Chinese. FECs come in denominations of 1, 5, 10, 50 and 100 *yuan* and 1 and 5 *jiao*. In addition to an engraving of a tourist mecca (the 100 *yuan* bill has the Great Wall, the 50 *yuan* has Elephant Trunk Hill in Guilin, the 1 *yuan* has Hangzhou's West Lake) on each bill, the value is given in Arabic numerals and complex Chinese accounting characters. The other side has 'Bank of China: Foreign Exchange Certificate' in English, and the amount again, this time in numerals and English.

There are periodic rumours that the Bank of China is planning to phase out the FECs, but at the time of writing no such action has been taken, or indeed seems likely.

RMB

The currency in general use is RMB. RMB comes in denominations of 1, 2, 5, 10, 50 and 100 *yuan* (the last two are fairly new, and as they represent a substantial sum to most Chinese, seldom seen), and 1, 2 and 5 *jiao*. These bills depict socialist images (workers, peasants and soldiers united on the 10 *yuan*, industrial workers on the 2 and 5), and the amount is given in accounting characters, romanization and Arabic numerals.

For amounts under one *jiao*, there are light silver-coloured 1, 2 and 5 *fen* coins and, less commonly, small bills for these amounts as well. Coins are shared by both currencies, but you may find that some places requiring payment in FECs are reluctant to accept them.

Cash purchases made in hotels, stores and restaurants catering to foreigners, as well as payment for taxis, should be in FECs. *Gongfei* students and resident foreigners with appropriate cards can substitute RMB in most cases, though for some products, such as silk, vendors may insist on FECs.

Since you can spend RMB at regular Chinese stores, on buses and in the markets, there is no problem for foreigners in accepting some – small RMB bills can be useful for shopping in town or for snacks – but only FECs can be exchanged for foreign currency when you leave China, so avoid accumulating too much RMB if you are not staying long.

Black market The two types of money are supposedly of equal value, but in fact FECs are much desired by Chinese citizens. FECs are needed to buy many high-demand imported items, and to shop at certain stores, clubs and restaurants, mainly catering to overseas Chinese, where RMB is not accepted. A conservative estimate of their street value is that 1 *yuan* FEC is worth 1.25 *yuan* RMB. There is an active black market in FECs, and also in Hong Kong and US dollars, which are required for buying foreign goods, as a hedge against inflation, and for travel or study abroad. (Both Hong Kong and US dollars are exchanged for about twice as much on the black market as at official outlets.) Young people will offer to change money outside hotels and in street markets. Changing money on the black market is illegal.

Credit cards Major hotels, Friendship Stores and antiques shops for foreigners take credit cards. All major foreign cards (American Express, Mastercard, Access, Visa etc.) are accepted. In addition, foreign customers of the Bank of China can be issued with the Bank's Great Wall credit card, which can be used in China only. A commission may be charged for cash advances on credit cards.

The number of businesses taking credit cards is increasing all the time, but smaller enterprises, and those in smaller centres, may well insist on cash. Cash is still required for purchasing air and rail tickets.

Traveller's cheques All major traveller's cheques are accepted in China. They can be readily exchanged for FECs at hotels, banks, Friendship Stores and points of entry.

Traveller's cheques are a safe way to carry money. For reasons of security, and because of the downward tendency of the *yuan*, they should be changed as needed rather than all at once on arrival in China. When buying traveller's cheques, find out from the issuing bank whom you should contact to have them replaced if they are lost while you are in China.

Banking

Foreigners resident in China can have accounts at the Bank of China. At local branches, accounts are in RMB; major branches will open accounts in FECs, US dollars, pounds sterling, Japanese yen and several European currencies. Money can be transferred to a Bank of China account from overseas, but it can be weeks before the branch acknowledges the transaction and credits the account. If you encounter such a delay, get the details of the transfer from the sender of the money, then indicate to your branch of the Bank of China that you will have to ask higher authorities to trace the missing money if it does not appear soon.

Over a hundred foreign banks have offices and branches in China. Most are in Beijing, but an increasing number are opening in the Special Economic Zones (see Business). To date, they have not been permitted to offer banking services to Chinese enterprises and individuals, but have concentrated on providing financial and import/export services, as well as business advice, to foreign businesses and Chinese-foreign Joint Ventures. The largest representation of a foreign bank in China is the Hongkong and Shanghai Bank, with four branches and three offices. Transfers between foreign banks and their branches in China can usually be completed in a business day.

Exercise and entertainment

The Chinese lifestyle is an energetic one. Only the wealthiest and most powerful travel by car. For the rest, walking and cycling provide plenty of exercise. Still, as anyone who has been in a Chinese park early in the morning will know, the Chinese also take recreational exercise seriously. Mid-morning breaks at schools, factories and offices are the time for the 'broadcast exercises' – simple calisthenics to music and instructions blaring from loudspeakers. For a couple of hours in the middle of the afternoon at schools and universities, classes stop while most students participate in some kind of sporting activity.

Foreign tourists in China may well feel that the activities that CITS organizes for them take up all the energy they have. Longer-term residents, especially those who go to a number of banquets, may want some exercise. Chinese cities cannot offer all the sporting facilities of a Western city, but it is usually possible to find enough to do to keep active.

Sightseeing In most Chinese cities, the past is everywhere. For those who were born there, old and often tumbledown pagodas and temples, tombs and arches, may be of minimal interest, but to the visitor, they are cause for exploration and delight. In China's ancient cities, such as Beijing and Xi'an, the Imperial past has left its mark; in Shanghai, Tianjin and Qingdao the heritage of colonialism is clearly visible; and in Chengdu, Suzhou and Hangzhou traditional Chinese society can be seen to endure. A strong and comfortable pair of shoes, a camera and one of the guide-books listed in the Further reading section are good for days of enjoyment. If you are heading out of the centre of town, a bicycle is an asset. Walkers and cyclists would do well to take a map, and if they speak no Chinese, the name of the place they want to visit and the place they are staying in Chinese on a piece of paper.

Zoos

There are zoos in Beijing, Shanghai, Guangzhou, and several other Chinese cities. The three named have pandas. Admission to Chinese zoos is very cheap (usually 40 *fen*), and there are usually lots of people there. One problem for foreign visitors is that they sometimes find themselves to be greater attractions than the animals!

Jogging

The athletic can jog, though this is not recommended for late risers. Most Chinese who run do so very early, before the worst of the traffic begins. The air in most Chinese cities is more polluted than that in New York or London, and running in it is liable to clog the bloodstream as well as pulverize the knees.

Martial arts

The preferred options, as can be seen in parks and roadsides, are the traditional martial arts, ranging from the slow and reflective *taijiquan* to more vigorous unarmed forms and exercises performed with swords, sticks and other weapons. Students and 'experts' at Chinese universities often have the opportunity to study *taijiquan*, though they may find their Chinese friends amused that they should have taken up an old person's activity in their youth.

Calisthenics and body-building

As well as doing the 'broadcast exercises', many Chinese now do an upbeat group calisthenics to rock music which looks a lot like Western aerobics. Jane Fonda's aerobics exercises are also popular (learned from translated texts rather than video-tapes) but they are seldom done in public places. The same is true of body-building. Magazines depicting Chinese and Western body-builders are hot sellers, both for fitness information and for titillation. Many young Chinese do body-building exercises, but they seldom work out where they can be seen.

Table-tennis

Table tennis is the sport for which China is best known. Tables can be found in clubs and schools, and makeshift games on concrete tables are played in village and city playgrounds. Tourists and visitors are sometimes invited to play against a local child barely tall enough to see over the table, who invariably turns out to have an unstoppable smash.

Pool and snooker

Snooker tables can still be found in some Chinese hotels. Some tables are accessible to the general public in former colonial haunts like the old Shanghai club on the Bund (Shanghai waterfront). Makeshift pool tables sprang up on city streets all over China following the general release of the Hollywood movie *The Colour of Money*, which featured Paul Newman as a pool player.

Other sports

Other commonly played team sports in a very sport-conscious country are basketball, volleyball and soccer, none of which need much equipment. Skating is popular in the north when the lakes freeze. Ice hockey is played in the north-east and by members of the foreign community in Beijing.

Building new sports facilities is a priority with the government, especially in the capital, the host city for the 1990 Asian Games. There is speculation that China will seek to host the Olympic Games in the year 2000 and is preparing the necessary facilities in advance.

Sports and the foreigner

Swimming pools and health clubs

Sports facilities catering to foreign visitors and residents have increased greatly in quality and range since the early 1980s. Many of the new international hotels offer their guests swimming pools, squash and tennis courts, and saunas; some (like the Shanghai Hilton) have health clubs that foreign residents can join. For long-term residents of the capital (preferably endowed with expense accounts), the Lido Centre on Jichang Road has indoor and outdoor tennis, squash, sauna and the other facilities of a top Western fitness club. The older International Clubs in Beijing (on Jianguomenwai Street) and Shanghai (65 Yan'an Road West) have pools and tennis courts on a pay-as-you-use basis.

Golf

There is a Japanese-built 18-hole golf course near the Ming Tombs outside Beijing, two more in

Zhongshan and Zhuhai in Guangdong province, and another outside Shanghai. A day's golfing is not cheap – at the Beijing course, a round of golf with rented clubs, cart, shoes and a caddie costs well over US$100. Reservations are needed for the weekend.

Entertainment

The years since the death of long-time Communist Party Chairman Mao Zedong and the ending of the Cultural Revolution in 1976 have seen a flourishing of the arts in China. Traditional entertainments formerly condemned as feudal and banned from Chinese stages have been revived. Renewed contact with the West has led both to a hunger for Western drama and music and to home-grown modern theatre and rock and roll.

Theatre

Opera The traditional Chinese dramatic form is opera, which has its origins in court entertainments performed for emperors over two thousand years ago. Operas combining song, drama, dance and acrobatics have been popular at least since the time of the Mongol occupation of north China in the thirteenth century.

Chinese opera is a highly stylized art-form, with a clearly defined repertoire of vocal techniques and symbolic gestures that performers must practise endlessly from an early age. Characters are defined not so much by their personalities as by the roles that they play in the drama. There are four main role types: the 'unpainted face' male characters, often scholars and judges; the 'painted face' military men; female characters (*ingénues*, maidservants and women warriors); and white-nosed 'clowns' who are as often sinister as comic.

Regional operatic forms not only reflect linguistic variations, but also feature different styles of singing and presentation. Best known is Beijing Opera, which was developed for court performance in the nineteenth century. It is now the dominant operatic form in China, and is characterized by its loud percussion and vigorous dramatic style. More melodious are the older *kunqu* from Suzhou and *yueju* from Guangdong. While Beijing Opera traditionally featured an all-male cast, Shaoxing Opera, which can often be seen in Shanghai, is performed by women.

Paper-cut of an opera figure: the woman warrior Mu Guiying

Some operas have modern or contemporary themes, but the best-loved pieces in the repertoire are probably the traditional stories, many of them derived from incidents in China's great classic novels. No concessions are made at the opera to non-speakers of Chinese (though those who can read Chinese will be glad to see the words to the arias projected onto screens beside the stage), but it is often possible to bone up on the story-line before you go. *Tales from Beijing Operas*, published in Beijing by New World Press, is a useful place to start. And a warning note – operas are long. Under two hours is unusual. Despite what guidebooks and some Chinese guides may tell you, it is impolite to get up and leave in the middle of a performance, particularly in a large group.

Spoken drama Spoken drama is not part of the Chinese tradition, and has only been staged in China since the early years of this century. It tends to be popular in times of increased interest in the West, flourishing in Shanghai and other major cities in the 1930s and 1940s, and again in the late 1970s and 1980s. In recent years, many foreign plays have been performed in Chinese on Beijing stages (including a Shakespeare festival and Arthur Miller's *Death of a Salesman*).

A vigorous Chinese theatre is developing, which is becoming increasingly daring in both social criticism and dramatic techniques. New plays in styles reminiscent of Brecht and Beckett are not always to the liking of the Communist Party authorities, who prefer the militant optimism of socialist realism. Knowledge of Chinese, or a willing and able interpreter, is an absolute necessity.

Variety shows Foreign visitors are often taken to evenings of variety entertainment. These can feature anything from modern dance numbers to Chinese romantic tenors singing 'O Sole Mio' and 'Rocky Mountain High', with a comedy routine thrown in as well.

Cinema

The Chinese are great movie-goers. In cinema, as in theatre, the range of permitted subject matter is increasing, and film-makers are becoming more adventurous and experimental in their direction of actors and cameramen. *Yellow Earth*, a stark tragedy of peasant life in China's north-west made in 1984, has been hailed as a breakthrough in Chinese film-making. Set in the 1940s, it portrays a young girl sold in marriage to an old man to finance the wedding of her younger brother. The film was shown abroad after surviving criticism by officials who found it too pessimistic and were annoyed that the Communist Party was not portrayed as solving all the peasants' problems.

Many Chinese films are made in subtitled versions, but these are mainly for showing abroad. If you plan to see Chinese films at local theatres, either ask friends or colleagues for a synopsis before going, or take an interpreter.

Some Western films are shown in China. Selection of which contemporary films are shown seems at times to be determined as much by the cost of their rights as by their success in the West, and films that did poorly at the box-office in North America can be big hits in China. Many film classics, such as the silent films of Charlie Chaplin, are familiar to Chinese audiences. Hollywood stars (Gregory Peck is one example) have recently become famous for films made many years ago, and are rapturously received when they make personal appearances before Chinese audiences.

Music

Traditional Concerts of Chinese music generally feature a series of short orchestral pieces interspersed with solos played on traditional instruments like the *pipa* (lute), *zheng* (zither), *erhu* (two-stringed fiddle), *sheng* (a multi-piped woodwind instrument) or bamboo flute. Blended ensembles of Chinese and Western instruments often accompany singers performing arrangements of Chinese and foreign songs.

Western classical China's older classical musicians were trained by the Russians in the 1950s. Western classical music was suppressed for much of the 1960s and 70s, but is now popular again. There are good orchestras in Beijing and Shanghai, and major Western orchestras and soloists visit China frequently.

Pop/rock Western and Chinese rock music is enormously popular with the young. The Hong Kong pop singer Theresa Teng was much admired in China in the early 1980s. Later, the American country singer

John Denver and the British pop group Wham! led the charge of foreign stars playing for Chinese audiences and filming themselves for the folks back home. As the 1990s begin, Michael Jackson and Madonna are popular favorites. The Communist Party warns periodically of the potentially corrupting effect of rock music on the young, but the damage may have been done already, as Chinese rockers are already established. One of them is Cui Jian, famous first with his group Adou and then as a solo performer, integrating Chinese melodies and instruments into Western rock. Cui's nihilistic lyrics had him banned from performance in 1987; then in 1990, his ten-city tour to raise money for the Asian Games was stopped half-way through by authorities uneasy with his style and message.

Ballet and dance

Chinese dancers perform ballet, modern dance and ponderous 'dance-dramas' on themes from Chinese history. Ballroom dancing is also becoming extremely popular in China, and foreigners are often asked to demonstrate foxtrots and tangos to Chinese friends at dances.

Circus and acrobatics

Other entertainments regularly available and much patronized by foreign visitors and residents are circus and acrobatic performances, and demonstrations of martial arts and gymnastics, in all of which the Chinese excel. Circus performers are human and animal, the animals including dogs, bears, the occasional tight-rope walking goat and the world's only performing panda (of the Shanghai Acrobatic Troupe), which sits in a cart pulled by dogs and blows a horn. The humans, many of them very young, perform prodigies of balancing, juggling and contortions.

Sporting events

China places great importance on sporting achievement, and sports heroes are lionized (though not paid) as much as their counterparts in the West. The old adage about 'friendship first, competition second' with which China re-entered international competition in the 1970s is now largely forgotten in the thrill of winning. Chinese athletes are world class in table tennis, gymnastics, diving, badminton and volleyball, and competitive in Asia in soccer and basketball. A more militantly partisan attitude to sports has led to crowd disturbances at soccer matches in recent years, though little to compare with a routine Saturday in England.

Tickets To find out what's on, check a newspaper. The English-language *China Daily* has listings, though almost exclusively for the capital. Tickets for entertainments tend to be in very heavy demand. Almost every film showing, concert and play has a full house. Most tickets are assigned in blocks to work-units, so the best bet is to get the unit in charge of you (for tourists, CITS) to arrange tickets. CITS also sells tickets for dramas and concerts to resident foreigners. Chinese people are used to lining up for several hours at awkward times to get tickets to sought-after events. If you have no ticket and do not mind paying a bit extra, there are often young ticket touts hawking tickets outside cinemas and theatres. Ticket prices are very reasonable by Western standards, even for celebrated visiting performers.

Nightlife

Hotels The time when the coffee-shop on the ground floor of the Beijing Hotel was the hub of diplomatic and government activity is now long past. There are coffee-shops and bars at most of the hotels that cater to tourists and businesspeople. In addition, many hotels now provide a dance floor for their guests and (in periods of relative liberality) for Chinese citizens from the upper stratum who have FECs to pay their cover charge. The usual name for these dance floors is *disike* (disco), and the music is generally upbeat, contemporary British or American.

For those with more sophisticated tastes who find themselves in Shanghai, the Peace Hotel on the Bund has a ground-floor bar with a band still composed at the time of writing of Chinese veterans of the jazz and swing bands that played for the Shanghailanders (foreign residents) in the 1940s. Expect to pay cover charges for entertainment, and Western club prices for drinks.

Outside

Foreign visitors who venture out of their hotels will find a nightlife which, though quiet by the standards of a Western city, is still more active than could ever have been imagined in the 1970s. The northern burghers of Beijing are more staid than their southern compatriots; the Shanghainese are livelier and the Cantonese liveliest of all. Quiet streets in those southern cities are more likely to indicate a popular Singaporean gangster series or classic serial on television than an early night for an exhausted citizenry.

New laws encouraging private enterprise have led to the opening of bars and clubs for Chinese customers, some staying open well into the night. These clubs range from small rooms with a couple of booths frequented by courting couples (the alternatives are doorways and park benches, which are always well patronized) to more elaborate nightspots, some of the grander of which are Joint Ventures involving outside investment. Restaurants and clubs offer afternoon tea-dances and evening *disike* for Chinese customers, with live and canned music. *Karaoke* is featured in some bars, whose customers can sing the syrupy ballads of Hong Kong and Taiwan to video images of endless beaches and girls in white dresses.

Prostitution

Urban unemployment, more money in circulation, and the influx of foreign businessmen have led to a resurfacing of prostitution on a large scale for the first time since the 1950s. Venereal diseases, and clinics to treat them, have also made a comeback. Avoid them all.

Television and radio

These are unpromising areas for the non-Chinese speaker. Chinese television is, naturally enough, mostly in Chinese, but there are frequent musical programmes which require little or no knowledge of the language, and an English-language programme called *English on Sunday*. If you intend to use a television and VCR in China you are advised to buy new equipment in Hong Kong. Chinese television runs on the signal PAL, which is incompatible with North American receivers. Chinese video-tapes cannot be played on standard North American VCRs. In Hong Kong it is possible to buy equipment that will handle both different television signals and any video-tapes you take in with you or borrow in China. Care should be exercised when taking videos into China: the Chinese have a lower threshold than most Westerners for pornography, and movies have been impounded by customs as offensive to Chinese morality.

There is much music, both Chinese and Western, on the radio. Programmes broadcast in English tend to be lessons in English for those contemplating the Test of English as a Foreign Language (TOEFL) needed for entry into most US and Canadian colleges. With a short-wave radio, you can join the millions of Chinese who listen daily to the morning broadcasts of the Voice of America and BBC World Service; Radio Canada International began broadcasting to China in 1988.

Beijing International Society

This society, run by foreign residents of the capital, arranges regular lectures on Chinese culture and history, and organizes other activities. There is a modest registration fee. The foreign residents of Shanghai also have an Expatriate Society.

Cuisine

'Have you eaten?' is a traditional greeting still heard in a country which has suffered many great famines over the centuries. Food has been important not only because of its scarcity, but also because China has developed one of the world's great cuisines. Most visitors will have tasted Chinese food before they arrive in China. However, the finest Chinatown meal can only suggest the wealth of tastes and textures that await the adventurous diner in China. There are delights for the eye, the nose and the palate, from refined delicacies once served only to emperors and princes to the hearty flavours of home cooking.

The five tastes

The many flavours of Chinese cooking are derived from five basic tastes: sweet, sour, savoury, spicy hot, and bitter. Each of these tastes is obtained through the use of appropriate ingredients – sugar or honey for sweet; vinegar for sour; salt or soy sauce for savoury; chilli peppers or chilli paste for spicy hot; and spring onions or bitter melons for bitter. In some dishes, one taste is dominant, as spicy hot is in the fiery dishes of western China. In others, there is a balance of tastes, as in sweet-and-sour dishes or hot-and-sour soup. If all five tastes are combined, they produce 'strange-taste' dishes.

Cooking methods

The cooking of most Chinese food is done in a limited number of ways. Meat (which is pork unless otherwise specified) is commonly stir-fried in very hot oil. The speed of the process economizes on fuel and oil, and the intense heat sterilizes meat which has probably not been refrigerated. Heavy use of oil in cooking is a sign of generous hospitality, and explains why many of the meals served to foreigners in China are rather too rich for some tastes. For deep-frying, more oil is used, but never as much as the pan of oil used for chip-making in the West.

Other methods of cooking include poaching (especially fish) and boiling or steaming (for rice, noodles and dumplings). Baking and roasting are less common, as few Chinese homes have ovens, but baked cakes and roast meat can be enjoyed in restaurants.

Regional cuisines

China is usually said to have four major regional cuisines (though styles of cooking, like dialects, can vary greatly from one locality to another even within a given region).

Northern

Northern or Mandarin cuisine is also known by the name of the capital Beijing. This region is known for its heavy sauces, many of them made with soyabean paste. Northern cooks use garlic liberally and those who live in this region are known to southerners for their garlic-scented breath.

The cooking of meat is strongly influenced by the Mongolian and Manchurian tastes. Mutton, uncommon in other parts of China, is used. Meat is often marinated before being cooked.

Perhaps the best known of northern dishes is Beijing Roast Duck, or Peking Duck. Specially force-fed ducks are inflated, basted and roasted. Slivers of the meat are wrapped with chopped spring onions and savoury sauce in thin flour-and-water pancakes. The combination of crispy skin, juicy fat and chewy meat, with the tang of onions and the richness of the sauce, is a taste and texture treat, though its richness is liable to loosen delicate stomachs. Because of the fame of Beijing Roast Duck and the numbers of people who want to eat it, the restaurants that serve it often bustle their customers unceremoniously through their meals.

A northern winter favorite is Mongolian hotpot. The diner places thin slices of mutton into stock that bubbles in a charcoal-heated pot placed at the centre of the table. When cooked, the meat is dipped into one of several strong condiments and eaten with sesame flavoured buns. It is a meal to warm the soul even on the coldest of nights.

Well-meaning restaurants and hotels in Beijing may attempt to favour the short-stay visitor with a meal that includes both Beijing Roast Duck and Mongolian hotpot. This is too much of a good thing, and may have the effect of putting the victim off both dishes for life. It is necessary to savour them one at a time.

The climate restricts the variety of vegetables available during the long, cold winters. Root crops such as potatoes, white turnips and swedes are generally stored after harvest in huge pits which protect them from frosts until they are dug up and used for winter cooking. For greens, northerners store Chinese cabbages in huge piles which freeze once winter comes. One of the sights of winter in the north is of truckloads of cabbages being driven to markets and mountains of frozen greens littering the ground. Increasingly, tomatoes are grown in energy-efficient greenhouses and are available well past normal growing seasons.

Southern

Southern or Cantonese is the Chinese cuisine with which most Westerners are familiar, since the majority of Chinese emigrants who have opened restaurants have been from Guangdong province. But Cantonese cooking in the West is a pale imitation of the real thing. In particular, the concoction known as 'chop suey' (the words mean 'smashed to pieces') is a nasty trick played only on foreigners, and unheard of in China.

Southern cooking is at once the most refined and the most adventurous of Chinese cuisines. Very fresh ingredients, especially seafoods, are lightly cooked and served in delicate sauces. Sometimes garlic and fermented black beans are used to provide stronger flavours. Southerners like to experiment with unusual blends of tastes, often combining seafood flavours like oyster sauce with meat. Sweet-and-sour is perhaps the most famous of southern tastes, though other regions have variants of it. For the Cantonese version, sugar and vinegar are blended in a fruit or vegetable base, most commonly a tomato paste.

Southerners have a reputation for being omnivorous: it is said that the Cantonese will eat anything with four legs except a table (stools have three legs), anything that flies except an aeroplane and everything that goes under water except a submarine.

Eastern Eastern cooking is characteristic of the region of the Yangtze river plain that includes Shanghai, Hangzhou and Nanjing and the smaller town of Yangzhou, for which the style of cooking is sometimes named. The region is rich in fresh-water fish, crabs and eels, as well as bamboo, a wealth of kinds of fungus and mushroom, and a glorious variety of vegetables. Sauces are not highly spiced but are prepared with a considerable amount of oil and rice-wine.

A common ingredient in the cooking of eastern China (and other regions) is *doufu* or beancurd (which the Japanese and many Westerners call *tofu*), a high-protein, gelatinous, white curd made of soyabeans. *Doufu* is an inexpensive and nutritious alternative to meat. It can also be bought in cake form, dried or fermented, in which case it is called *chou doufu*, 'stinking beancurd', and smells a bit like ripe Gorgonzola cheese.

Sichuan/ Hunan Chinese cuisine from the provinces of Sichuan and Hunan is known for its copious use of chilli peppers. Ginger and, indicative of its northern origins, garlic are often used as well. The strong flavours were developed in part to disguise the salt, pickling or smoking that were used to preserve meat and fish.

Not all of the dishes of Hunan and Sichuan are peppery-hot, but since this is the taste for which the region is famed, it is the dominant theme in this book's one recipe, a noble dish called Gongbao Chicken.

Chefs are most adept at cooking the specialities of their native region. In Beijing and Shanghai, towns with a cosmopolitan tradition, good food representative of other areas is available, but in most places the local favourites are likely to be the best. The Cantonese, with their delicate palates, are especially reluctant to reproduce the mouth-numbing sauces of western China, which accounts for the blandness of the food at many of the so-called Hunan and Sichuan restaurants that have opened outside China.

Chinese meals The Chinese meal consisting of rice and a variety of dishes that most Westerners know from Chinese restaurants is typically eaten as an evening meal.

Grains

The principal constituent of every Chinese meal is grain. In south China, the staple is rice, which is served boiled, steamed, stir-fried or ground into flour to make vermicelli. In the north, where the climate does not favour rice cultivation, wheat and coarser grains like millet, sorghum and corn meal are eaten. Wheat is ground into flour for use in making noodles, buns, pancakes or the Western-style bread that has become more common in recent years. Rice and wheat can be found throughout China now, but traditional preferences remain strong.

Dishes

'Dishes' complement the staple grain. For a humble meal, a few pickled vegetables may be piled onto a bowl of rice or noodles. A family meal or a restaurant meal will have a selection of dishes arranged in the centre of the dining table. On more formal occasions, the dishes arrive one at a time so that each one can be savoured separately. Diners have their own bowl of rice or noodles, and serve themselves from the dishes. A boarding-house reach is an asset.

At formal meals, the host may serve guests first, and continue to pile food on their plates until the guests plead that such politeness is unnecessary and that they should all take their own food. Rice is served only at the end of banquets – the host is supposed to provide so much in the way of rich dishes that the guest does not need to fill up on plain rice.

Meals are typically washed down with a bowl of soup, though beer is a popular alternative in restaurants. Drinking tea with a Chinese meal is not common inside China. Dessert is not usually served, though Chinese chefs make delicious sweet dishes. Fruit is sometimes offered to clean the palate.

Breakfast

A Chinese breakfast is generally regarded by those Chinese who deal with foreigners to be quite unsuited to Western tastes. It is true that those used to a Western diet can find a triple daily dose of rice hard on the system (or, more specifically, constipating), but breakfast is worth a try.

The main constituent, *zhou* or rice-gruel, is a warm stomach-filler. Flavouring is provided by adding pickled vegetables, salted fish, or cold meat. In the north-east, *zhou* is replaced by a porridge made of millet or sorghum, or by heavy buns of corn meal called *wotou*. Another type of Chinese breakfast consists of hot soyabean milk, which is served either sweet or savoury (with pickles and hot-sauce). It is usually accompanied by long doughnut sticks and hard sesame cakes. Just describing this breakfast makes the author of this chapter salivate uncontrollably.

Lunch Although the midday meal served to travellers is often similar to the evening meal, midday is also the ideal time to sample dumplings and pastries which are known collectively as *dianxin*, sometimes translated as 'heart's delight'. In the West these delicacies are known as *dimsum* (Cantonese pronunciation), and many people will be familiar with them from Chinatown lunches.

One type of *dianxin* that can be found throughout the country is the meat-filled dumpling. The Beijing version is called *jiaozi*: a filling made of ground pork and/or beef combined with Chinese chives, ginger and garlic is wrapped in round 'skins' of dough, pinched shut and then boiled or steamed. When made with leavened dough, the dumplings are called *baozi*. Fried *jiaozi* are called *guotie*, 'potstickers', and fried *baozi* are called *shengjian mantou*. Dumplings boiled and served in soup are called *huntun*. Everyday dumplings are large; the more refined ones are designed to go into the mouth in one bite, which is just as well since juicy dumplings can make a nasty mess of one's clothing unless eaten carefully. In Shanghai and its environs the soup-filled *xiaolong bao*, 'little dragon' dumpling, is favoured. Similar dumplings made in the northern city of Tianjin rejoice in the name *goubuli*, 'dogs won't bother with them'. The Cantonese are masters of dumpling cookery. Their varieties include *hah gao* (shrimp dumplings) and spring rolls, a version of which can be found in almost every Chinese restaurant outside China.

A warning about the midday meal – most Chinese follow it with a *xiuxi* or nap of a couple of hours. A large meal of *dianxin* can have an anaesthetic effect!

Chopsticks

Chinese food is eaten with chopsticks. While chopsticks seem intimidating to the first-time user, a couple of days' practice is usually all that is required for efficient, though perhaps not elegant, eating.

There are two basic chopstick techniques: picking, for which one chopstick is held rigid between thumb and middle finger while the index finger guides the other chopstick; and scooping, for which the chopsticks are both held rigid about half an inch apart and rice is lifted to the mouth in lumps. Holding the rice-bowl above the level of the table is a socially acceptable way of lessening the distance between food and mouth. The bowl can even be lifted to mouth level to finish the remaining grains of rice.

People who eat in Chinese university canteens may be surprised to see fellow diners using spoons to eat their meals. Spoons are considered more efficient than chopsticks for consuming food in the shortest possible time, though a foreigner who has attempted to eat a whole pork chop balanced on a spoon may contest this.

How to make Gongbao Chicken
(slightly adapted, with the author's permission, from *The Good Food of Szechwan* by Robert A. Delfs)

According to legend, when a certain Ding Gongbao received an appointment as an imperial official to Sichuan, he prepared a dinner for his friends that included this dish, which became known by his name. Gongbao Chicken, in one form or another, is one of the best known and most often prepared Sichuanese foods. Whole dried peppers are purposely cooked until they are burnt, flavouring the oil in which the chicken is to be cooked. The final dish should be somewhat sweet, slightly spicy and also hot from the charred red chilli peppers of which there should be an adequate supply. Be careful when you cook this dish because the volatile oil of red peppers tends to be released into the air while the peppers are cooking. If you don't have a range-hood or exhaust-fan over your stove, open all the windows and keep doors to other rooms closed while charring the peppers.

Ingredients:

½ chicken breast, about 250 g (½ lb) when boned

Marinade:

2 tsps cornflour (cornstarch)
2 tsps soy sauce
1 tbsp. rice-wine or dry sherry
½–1 egg white
½ tsp. salt

10 dried red chilli peppers, or a few more
2 tsps finely chopped fresh ginger
1 spring onion (green onion)
¼ cup cashews, or peanuts or almonds

Seasonings:
2 tsps cornflour (cornstarch)
2 tsps rice-wine or dry sherry
1–2 tbsps soy sauce
1 tsp. vinegar
½ tsp. salt (omit if using salted nuts)
1–2 tsps sugar
2 tsps sesame oil (optional)

4 tbsps oil

To prepare:

1 Bone the chicken breast and cut the meat into small cubes.

2 To make the marinade, mix the cornflour with 2 tsps soy sauce and 1 tbsp. wine, then add the salt and egg white. Mix the marinade with the chicken and marinate for at least 15 minutes.

3 Cut off the ends of the dried red peppers and shake out the seeds. Chop the ginger very finely and cut the spring onions into 2 cm (¾ inch) lengths.

4 Mix the seasonings in a small bowl by first combining the cornflour with the soy sauce and wine and then mixing in the other ingredients.

To cook:

1 Heat about 4 tbsps cooking oil in a wok or large frying pan. Add the red peppers, and cook over a medium heat until they start to char. Turn the heat up as high as possible and as soon as the peppers are black, add the chicken pieces. Reduce heat to medium.

2 Stir-fry until the chicken is white, then add the ginger and spring onion. Cook, stirring for a few more seconds, then add the cashews or other nuts and the seasonings (give them a quick stir first). When the sauce has thickened slightly and is glaze-like, remove to a serving-dish and serve hot.

Eating and drinking

The culinary delights described in the previous chapter can be sampled in hotels and restaurants large and small across the country. At hotels and restaurants accustomed to dealing with foreigners, menus will generally be in both English and Chinese. For those who speak and read no Chinese, trying out smaller and more out-of-the-way restaurants represents a leap into the dark, but one that can reward the daring with experiences and tastes to savour for years to come.

Special diets Sticking to special diets can present difficulties, especially for those moving from town to town, but it is not impossible. Although they do not always accept the reasons for doing so, chefs will often, given sufficient notice, omit the flavour-enhancer monosodium glutamate and cut down on their use of oil. Diners who for dietary or religious reasons do not wish to eat pork can have pork dishes identified and avoid them, though they should be aware that the oil used in other dishes may contain some pork-fat. Alternatively, they can seek out Muslim (*Huimin*) restaurants, which serve no pork and cook with vegetable oil, or eat in vegetarian restaurants. While maintaining a special diet is more difficult for people travelling in group tours, it is often possible for a tour leader to arrange to have steamed fish, a *doufu* or vegetable dish, or eggs scrambled in vegetable oil cooked for you. Boiled noodles are an option, though many people balk at a steady diet of them. If you have special dietary requirements, you should prepare yourself with a supply of snacks for those occasions when appropriate meals cannot be found.

Health concerns Standards of hygiene are lower away from hotels and restaurants that cater principally to foreigners.

Tables and floors at low-cost eateries can be strewn with debris from other diners by the end of mealtime. Public health officials make periodic inspections, but standards remain lower than many foreigners find acceptable. Eating utensils are sometimes only rinsed clean rather than being sterilized, which presents an unacceptable risk during hepatitis epidemics like the one that swept east-central China in 1988. Chinese travellers of the past carried their own chopsticks, and many now do so again. The foreign diner may choose to follow their example.

Smoking

Many Chinese men smoke a lot, and have only recently been alerted to the health risks involved. Smoking in restaurants is common and Chinese restaurants do not as a rule have non-smoking sections. However, if you tell a waiter or waitress that cigarette smoke makes you ill, he or she may try to keep smokers away from you. Delivering loud lectures on the evils of smoking will do no good.

Eating out

Banquets and meals organized in advance are ordered according to a *biaozhun* or standard price, for which the restaurant provides an appropriate meal. The *biaozhun* does not normally include drinks, and a service charge and room rental charge may also be added. Most restaurants operate the same principle as the airlines and railways – standard prices for foreigners are about double what the same meal would cost a Chinese person.

Tourists travelling in groups are provided with meals based on a *biaozhun* which CITS pays hotels. If most members of a group choose to eat a meal out of their hotel, a guide can often arrange to have the *biaozhun* transferred from the hotel to a restaurant. Extra charges above the *biaozhun* are borne by the diners.

Choosing a restaurant

Guidebooks have listings of major hotels and restaurants, some with suggestions of how much a meal can be expected to cost. Allow generously for inflation, even when using the most recent editions of the guidebooks. Prices of meals at top restaurants are comparable to those you might pay for a similar meal in the West.

For a less expensive alternative: if you find a restaurant on the street which appeals, just walk in. Restaurants are cleaner and a little less busy if you go at or just before opening time. Hours for restaurants which do not usually cater to foreigners are early: something like 6.00–8.00 for breakfast, 11.00–12.30 for lunch and 5.00–7.30 for dinner. You may be offered an inner room – even restaurants that seldom see foreigners have private rooms for officials – or you can choose to eat in the main dining area, where you will have to share a table if your numbers are not enough to fill it. If you arrive well into a mealtime, you will probably have to wait. The Chinese practice in this situation is to select a table where the meal is almost finished and stand over it to stake a claim and encourage the present occupants to eat up. Zealous waiters may try to hurry diners from their meal so that the foreign guests can sit down to theirs, but they should be discouraged from doing so. If you want to eat with the people, you should be prepared to wait with the people.

Many privately-run restaurants have opened since the early 1980s. These range from small family-run businesses to elaborate ventures with floor-shows and waiters in bow-ties. In many cases service and food are of a higher standard, and opening hours much longer than in state-run restaurants.

Numerous small noodle- and snack-shops and other food vendors can be found along the streets of Chinese cities and towns. No language is necessary – pointing for selection and sign-language for quantity and price are enough.

Finding Western food

Most visitors to China decide to eat Chinese food at some times and Western food at others. This can be easily arranged. Non-international hotels assume that tourists will eat a Western breakfast and Chinese food at lunch and dinner, but will provide Western lunches and dinners if requested to do so (a day's notice is sometimes needed).

The quality of Western food is higher in towns with a longer tradition of foreign residence and tourism. The largest and most modern hotels built in the 1980s

"Of course, some of the sense of wonder and mystery disappears when you find that it's the local McDonald's."

Reproduced by courtesy of *Punch*

work on the principle that international travellers and businesspeople should be able to enjoy in China all the comforts and luxuries of a first-class hotel anywhere else in the world, and the Western food is as it should be in such a setting.

The most celebrated Western restaurant in China is Maxim's in Beijing, owned by Yves St Laurent and opened in 1983. Food, wine, service and prices are appropriately Parisian. At the other end of the scale, the same city has the world's largest Kentucky Fried Chicken franchise.

In the former foreign enclaves of Shanghai and Tianjin, the visitor can find Western restaurants set up in the 1930s and 1940s, which have survived the ups and downs of forty years of Chinese socialism and now find themselves in vogue again. Western dishes from hamburger and goulash to chicken Kiev have been adapted to Chinese tastes at Red House (formerly Chez Louis) and Deda (formerly the Cosmopolitan), both in Shanghai, at Tianjin's Cafe Kiesling and at many other restaurants.

Smaller independently run restaurants and bars in Chinese cities often have a Western theme. Expect good ice-cream, cakes that range from acceptable to superb, and variable coffee. Also expect to see China's young and trendy among your fellow-customers.

Bakeries selling Western-style bread operate in many Chinese cities, and cannot produce enough to satisfy the demand, even at prices which many find hard to afford.

Eating as a guest

Visitors to Chinese homes or farming communities are often told, with the deprecation of Chinese good manners, that they will be served only *bianfan* (ordinary food). Home-cooked *bianfan* can be Chinese food at its very best, with the freshest ingredients and most careful preparation. Enthusiastic appreciation is usually merited and always welcomed. If eating with Chinese friends in their homes, a gift of fruit, sweets or something to drink is appropriate.

Institutional eating

Institutional food in China, such as is served to foreign students and teachers at colleges and universities, is like institutional food everywhere – adequate, convenient and dull. Institutions with foreign residents usually set up a special dining room for them, where the food is rich in meat and oil and costs restaurant prices. Those who prefer to eat with Chinese fellow-students and colleagues will find the food in their canteens neither very nutritious nor very tasty. Universities are often supplied with rice that has been stored a long time, is tasteless and has pieces of grit in. (One of the authors broke a tooth on institutional rice.) Meals at Chinese canteens are eaten quickly, often standing up, from bowls supplied by the diner. The canteen diet is one which should, for gastronomic and nutritional reasons, be supplemented with fruit and meals bought off-campus, or by self-catering.

Cooking for yourself

Foreign teachers and students are provided with basic cooking facilities, most often a couple of gas rings. Utensils can be taken along, or bought inexpensively in China. The basic necessity is the round-bottomed, high-sided *guo* pan (known in the West by its Cantonese name, wok). The ones with a single, long, wooden handle are more manageable than those with two small metal handles, and a lid is needed for boiling or steaming. Kettles are provided for boiling water.

Ingredients can be bought at the free markets. Meat is less packaged than the Western buyer is used to – for example, chickens are often sold live, which makes for unaccustomed work in food preparation. Vegetables should be washed thoroughly and not eaten raw, since they are fertilized with animal and human excrement. All fruit should be peeled.

If you plan to cook for yourself, take a couple of favourite cookbooks, and also some of the herbs and spices you like to use, since not all will be readily available (even if you know where to buy them and how to ask for them!). A measuring cup and measuring spoons are useful if you are planning to do any baking.

Drinking

The Chinese are not as a rule great drinkers of alcohol. Women drink very occasionally, and men are more likely to drink to celebrate something than as a social activity. This is not to say that the Chinese disdain alcohol – the great poetry of Chinese antiquity was as much inspired by yeast sediment as high sentiment. Even today, many people believe in the restorative powers of a shot of the hard stuff, especially if some ginseng or other tonic has been soaking in it.

Spirits Distilled spirits of rice and other grains have a long tradition in China. The best known abroad is the strikingly packaged and grossly overpriced *maotai*, but other less celebrated spirits are all but indistinguishable in taste. The less refined *baiganr*, which costs pennies a glass at local restaurants, can warm the spirit and sear the throat just as well as *maotai*. The Chinese make a drinkable brandy and versions of other familiar spirits, which should only be tried by the inquisitive and desperate.

Beer Beer is one of the most fortunate legacies of colonialism in China, and is sufficiently popular that supply can seldom keep up with demand. China's most famous beer is named after the place where it is produced, the north-eastern city of Qingdao (or Tsingtao). The brewery was set up during the German occupation of Shandong province in the early part of this century, and uses the mineral waters of the Laoshan spring. Recently Joint Ventures with foreign breweries have put new brands on the Chinese markets, including the excellent Chinese-Dutch Reeb brand produced in Shanghai. Elsewhere the beer is generally good, and not too strong for the easily influenced. Colour and degree of bitterness seem to vary from batch to batch of the local brews rather than between brands. Draft beer, uncarbonated and sometimes cloudy, is available at humbler eating establishments. Dark beer can occasionally be found and is likely to please the English beer-drinker.

Wines Grape wine is a relatively new product in China. Early attempts at making wine, mostly red, resulted in products that were syrupy and almost undrinkable. In recent years, a Joint Venture with French partners has produced drier white wines, including one labelled Great Wall. The indigenous wines are yellow rice-wines, which taste like a sweet sherry and are drunk warm. They enter the bloodstream quickly and can give a powerful hangover.

Imported drinks Imported wines and spirits are available in Friendship Stores, and at stores and bars in hotels at prices comparable to those in Europe or North America. Selection is reasonable. Coca-Cola, Pepsi-Cola, and

Sprite are available in more or less every city, and many hotels have other Western soft drinks and mineral waters.

Non-alcoholic

Mineral water can be drunk at many hotels and restaurants. The best-known brand is Laoshan, but this is not always available, especially in south China.

Chinese carbonated drinks come in two main types – cola, which tastes more or less like Western ones, and orange soda, which is vivid orange in colour, entirely artificial in taste and even worse warm than cold. Fruit juices and soya-milk are sold in individual-sized tetrapack cartons. Fresh orange juice can be bought at some Friendship Stores.

Teas

Tea is drunk at meetings, on visits to factories and at almost all social occasions. Most Chinese hotel rooms have large thermos flasks of boiled water which can be used to make tea, and many also supply tea-bags or leaves. Three basic categories of tea are:

- green tea, which is the dried leaves of the tea-bush, and has all the original flavour of the leaf. China's most famous tea, Longjing or Dragonwell, is a green tea.
- black tea (the Chinese call it 'red tea'), which is made of leaves roasted to a flavour more familiar to Western tea-drinkers.
- 'flower tea', which is black tea to which flowers or other flavouring have been added. Jasmine and chrysanthemum are common varieties.

Tea is most often made by adding boiling water to leaves in a cup, rather than being brewed in a pot. If the cup has a lid, leave it on for a while and the leaves will sink to the bottom. This makes drinking the tea a quieter and cleaner process than it can ever be if sucked through floating leaves and teeth.

Boiled water, sometimes called white tea, is generally available. Cold boiled water can sometimes be had on request. Tap-water should not be drunk anywhere in China, or even be used for teeth-cleaning.

Holidays and festivals

Two calendars
Gregorian

China has adopted the Western Gregorian calendar for official purposes. Holidays and festivals with modern origins are celebrated according to this calendar. Public holidays are on New Year's Day, 1 January; International Women's Day, 8 March (time off for women only); and Labour Day, 1 May. National Day is on 1 October, the anniversary of the proclamation of the establishment of the People's Republic of China in 1949, and begins a two-day holiday. Other events with political significance are commemorated, though they are not public holidays. These include Youth Day on 4 May, which is the anniversary of the nationalist demonstrations of 1919 (see A look at the past); and the anniversaries of the founding of the Communist Party and the People's Liberation Army, on 1 July and 1 August respectively.

The Gregorian calendar coexists with the traditional Chinese calendar, which is based primarily on the lunar cycle. Dates in both the Gregorian and traditional systems appear on Chinese calendars.

The Farmer's Calendar

The traditional calendar is known as the Xia (after the prehistoric dynasty in which it is believed to have been devised) or the Farmer's Calendar. Months in the Farmer's Calendar are of 29 or 30 days, so the 12 months of most years do not complete the 365 ¼ days of the earth's rotation. The shortfall is made up by adding an extra month seven out of every nineteen years. It is impossible to guess which dates on the Gregorian calendar the lunar festivals will fall on without a calendar or almanac.

The almanac, which advises Chinese readers the world over on lucky and unlucky days for such diverse activities as marriage, travel and haircuts, follows the

Farmer's Calendar, as do the traditional festivals which have punctuated and enlivened the Chinese year for two millennia.

Traditional festivals

The main festivals of the Chinese year are described below. For a fuller list, see *Folk Customs at Traditional Chinese Festivities*, published in Beijing by Foreign Languages Press.

Spring Festival

New Year in the Farmer's calendar, now called Spring Festival to distinguish it from 1 January, falls somewhere between 21 January and 20 February. It is the most important festival of the Chinese year. Spring Festival is the occasion for family reunions and celebration. The standard holiday is three days long, but people working far from home are given more time off to allow them to rejoin their families. Spring Festival is also the time when hundreds of thousands of Hong Kong residents and overseas Chinese visit their relatives on the mainland. Offices are closed and trains more than usually packed. Avoid trying to do business or travel during Spring Festival.

In past years, Spring Festival was an anxious time for China's poor, since it was a day by which debts had to be paid. Peasants who owed money would go into hiding from their landlords' bailiffs until daybreak on the first day of the new year, as debts were not collected over the holiday.

The last day of the old year is the occasion for both the biggest house-cleaning and the greatest feast of the year in Chinese homes. Fish is generally eaten, since the word for 'fish', *yu*, has the same sound as 'abundance'; so 'fish every (new) year' is a wish for 'abundance every year'. Pieces of sticky New Year's cake are also eaten. A traditional practice, more common in the countryside, is to present offerings of food to family ancestors and to gods of the household and the land. Firecrackers let off to drive away evil spirits send out the old year and usher in the new on a deafening note.

During the Spring Festival period, many families put up colourful New Year pictures, which depict such promising images as fish, plump babies and bountiful harvests. They also hang strips of paper, red for luck, and inscribed with suitably auspicious sentiments, on either side of the front door. Children may receive gifts of money from their parents in 'red packages'. The festival is a happy time of family celebration and public enjoyment of lion-dances and other such street entertainments.

Lantern Festival

Spring Festival is concluded at the first full moon of the year, on the fifteenth day of the first month, with the Festival of Lanterns. Paper and silk lanterns in a variety of shapes and colours are hung outside houses. The Lantern Festival, like most Chinese festivities, has a food associated with it. Heavy dumplings are made of glutinous rice flour stuffed with a variety of sweet fillings. In Beijing these are called *yuanxiao*, which is the Chinese name for the festival as well as the food.

Festival of Graves

One of the festivals of the Chinese year that is reckoned according to the solar calendar is *Qingming* ('clear and bright'), the Festival of Graves, which falls on 4 or 5 April. This is the day that family graves are tidied and decorated in an expression of respect for the dead. Cremation is now the rule in Chinese cities, so urbanites have no graves to attend to, but they can still use the festival to commemorate the dead, both family members and national heroes.

Dragon-boat Festival

The fifth day of the fifth lunar month is the occasion for noisy and exciting rowing races between teams of oarsmen in dragon-boats – narrow vessels with dragons' heads on their prows. Dragon-boat racing, banned for many years as a feudal practice, is once again popular in rural China. The dragons on the boats are supposed to subdue the dragons that are believed to live in China's rivers and cause flooding.

The festival commemorates the suicide by drowning of the poet and statesman Qu Yuan in 278 BC to protest against a ruler who unwisely ignored his advice. A traditional food for the dragon-boat festival is a steamed ball of glutinous rice with meat, savoury and sweet ingredients wrapped in bamboo leaves.

Mid-autumn Festival

At the autumn equinox, on the fifteenth day of the eighth lunar month, when the moon is at its brightest, the Chinese celebrate the Mid-autumn or Moon Festival. Traditionally, people gather to enjoy the beauties of the moon and moonlit scenery. A common image associated with this time is the rabbit, after a jade rabbit said in a Buddhist legend to live in the moon. Sweet decorated cakes, called moon-cakes, are eaten.

What's your Chinese sign?

Each year in the Chinese lunar calendar is associated with one of twelve animals. The year of your birth identifies you with one of those animals, and this is believed to determine your personality and should influence your choice of marriage partner. Superstitious Chinese men often avoid women born in the years of the dragon or tiger; they may be too hard to handle! Here is a list of years, their animals and a couple of qualities associated with each.

Years	*Animal*	*Qualities*
1900, 1912, 1924, 1936, 1948, 1960, 1972, 1984	Rat	Ambitious, tempera-mental
1901, 1913, 1925, 1937, 1949, 1961, 1973, 1985	Ox	Easy-going, inspiring
1902, 1914, 1926, 1938, 1950, 1962, 1974, 1986	Tiger	Courageous, sensitive
1903, 1915, 1927, 1939, 1951, 1963, 1975, 1987	Rabbit	Lucky, talented
1904, 1916, 1928, 1940, 1952, 1964, 1976, 1988	Dragon	Excitable, stubborn

1905, 1917, 1929, 1941, 1953, 1965, 1977, 1989	Snake	Intense, determined
1906, 1918, 1930, 1942, 1954, 1966, 1978, 1990	Horse	Cheerful, impetuous
1907, 1919, 1931, 1943, 1955, 1967, 1979, 1991	Sheep	Creative, timid
1908, 1920, 1932, 1944, 1956, 1968, 1980, 1992	Monkey	Inventive, influential
1909, 1921, 1933, 1945, 1957, 1969, 1981, 1993	Rooster	Pioneering, eccentric
1910, 1922, 1934, 1946, 1958, 1970, 1982, 1994	Dog	Loyal, generous
1911, 1923, 1935, 1947, 1959, 1971, 1983, 1995	Pig	Affectionate, irascible

How to find your sign

If you were born on or after 21 February, simply locate the year of your birth on the chart above. If your birthday is in the first twenty days of January, you are said to have been born in the 'tail' of the preceding year's animal. People born between 21 January and 20 February must consult a Chinese almanac to discover when the lunar new year fell in the year of their birth. If it was before their birthday, they can pick their year from the chart above. If lunar new year came after their birthday, then they are in the preceding animal's tail.

Shopping

There is plenty to buy in China, and there are plenty of people anxious to sell it. Forty per cent of the country's income from tourism is derived from retail sales, a large proportion of that being in arts and crafts. A wide variety of antiques, copies of ancient works and modern pieces can be bought; in fact, most of the arts and crafts now produced are for export or sale to visitors. In addition to these products, visitors can take home many useful and distinctive household articles. Foreign residents will also need to shop for food and daily necessities.

If you are not yet used to Chinese money, it is a good idea to sort out large and small bills before you go out. If you have any RMB, keep it separate, and use it for purchases made away from stores catering exclusively to foreigners.

Where to shop

Hotels

All hotels have shops, ranging from modest outlets selling postcards, stamps and souvenirs to fully fledged shopping arcades in larger and newer hotels. Among the most extensive of these arcades is the one at the Holiday Inn Lido in Beijing, where shops include a Western delicatessen.

Friendship Stores

Towns open to foreign tourists invariably have at least one Friendship Store stocking clothing, arts and crafts, antiques, some luxury foods, stationery and souvenirs, plus imported drinks, cigarettes and film, for the convenience of visitors to China. Friendship Stores also generally carry some local speciality products as well as the standard fare. Items in Friendship Stores are paid for in FECs, and generally cost a little more than comparable ones in a Chinese department store, but for this premium the customer gets a much greater variety of goods at the upper end of the scale (for example, more choice of silk shirts than synthetics or cotton/synthetic blends). It is also possible to change money at most Friendship Stores.

Chinese shops

Foreign residents and tourists should also visit ordinary Chinese shops to get an idea of what is available and popular with Chinese consumers. Be ready for crowds: to give one extreme example, Shanghai's Number 1 Department Store, very near the Park Hotel on Nanjing Road, is as crowded every weekday as a Western department store the first day of the January sales, and on Sundays it gets really busy! Shopping in town involves more walking, and takes longer, than shopping in a Friendship Store, but it is easier on the finances and more interesting.

Factory outlets

Factories making carpet, silks, *cloisonné* and porcelain, and centres producing handicrafts, all have shops selling their products. Almost everywhere something is made and foreigners visit, there is a chance to buy. Prices are not necessarily lower than at Friendship Stores, but selection can be very good, and a souvenir or gift often has greater significance for having been bought at the place it was produced.

Antique shops

Antiques shops and official shops at historical sites sell antique and reproduction furniture, porcelain, handicrafts and jewellery. Nothing over 100 years old can be exported, so everything you buy will be late Qing at the earliest (see A look at the past). Antiques approved for export have an official seal on them, usually attached to the price-tag. This must be left on, and your sales-receipt must be retained, for clearing customs on your departure. The supply of antiques, though large, is finite, and the demand for them seems to be infinite. Prices are often higher than in Hong Kong or the West, so unless you are very knowledgeable, buy for pleasure rather than as an investment.

Markets

Antique and clothing markets can be found in larger cities. The 'antiques' are considerably cheaper than at the government outlets, and range from the genuinely valuable to amusing bric-a-brac. At clothing markets, you can buy Chinese-made Western designer clothes at a fraction of the usual price.

Free markets selling food are of particular interest to foreign residents who make their own meals. Food tends to be fresher and more varied than in the state-run private markets, though a bit more expensive. The greatest variety of all is to be found in the markets of Guangzhou, a result of the Cantonese taste for the exotic.

Other goods to be found in the markets are cassette-tapes, cigarettes, haberdashery, souvenirs and whatever else anyone has to sell. Bargaining is the rule, though of course the vendors will be happy if you pay the first price they ask. Even the most skilled and persistent foreign haggler will end up paying more than a Chinese customer, but the differential can be kept low. Vendors hope that foreigners will pay in FECs, but will also quote a higher price in RMB. Tailors, cobblers and barbers also ply their trade in the markets.

When shopping in the markets, bear in mind that in China it is the purchaser, and not the vendor or the market management, that checks the quality of the goods sold. *Caveat emptor*!

What to buy

Textiles

Natural fibres, particularly silk and cotton, are readily available at stores for foreigners. (Wool and cashmere have gone up in price and are no longer the bargains they once were.) Materials are good quality and less expensive than in the West. Raw silk, available in the silkworm-raising area around Shanghai, Suzhou and Hangzhou, is a beautiful fabric, less common in the West than more processed silks. In the north and south-west you can buy cotton batik, usually in blue and white.

Clothing

Clothes are usually well made, though styles and sizes can be limited. At shops in town, easy-care synthetics and cotton/synthetic blends are more common than pure natural fibres, and more practical for Chinese buyers, few of whom have irons. Chinese people tend to wear shirts and blouses looser than most Westerners, but are generally slimmer. Sizes can be a problem for tall or large people. As well as whites and plain colours, you can buy clothing in colours bright to the point of garishness.

Clothes can be expertly made up from patterns or by copying your own favourites. There are tailors working at some Friendship Stores, at state-run textile shops, and at privately operated establishments. Having clothes made takes more time than most tourists have at one place, and is consequently recommended only for longer-term residents.

Books

Chinese books in English, and some imported books, are available at hotel bookshops and at sections reserved for foreign customers in large branches of the New China Bookstore (*Xinhua Shudian*). The *China Guides* series of guidebooks, produced in Hong Kong and covering different regions of China, is generally available and very useful. You can also buy books published in China on Chinese history, geography, law, cuisine, art and more besides. Recommended for lovers of fiction are the small paperback Panda Books, which are mostly translations of classical and contemporary literature. Popular contemporary authors whose work has been much translated include Wang Meng (Minister of Culture from 1983 to 1989), Gu Hua, Zhang Xianliang and Zhang Jie. Chinese fiction of the 1980s, besides being of interest as literature, is also a good guide to changes and issues in Chinese society, especially among the 'intellectual class' to which most authors belong.

Household goods

Residents and tourists without too many constraints on luggage space should be on the lookout for interesting household articles, which can be bought inexpensively in hardware and specialized shops. Cooking utensils, kitchen cleavers and big thermos bottles are the staples of life in China and useful outside as well. Mugs with lids are fine for drinkers of coffee as well as Chinese tea. Teapots, in materials ranging from porcelain to terracotta, come in all shapes and sizes, in styles which can be elegant, ornate or kitsch.

Arts and crafts

Paintings

Paintings, usually mounted on scrolls, are available everywhere at a range of prices. Most works are designed to appeal to what the artists consider foreign

'Shaking the money tree' by Jing He and Jing Guo

taste to be. Commonest are works in the familiar 'national style', many of them landscapes, which can be relied on to depict mountains, water, buildings and human figures. Prices often reflect the seniority and institutional standing of the artist as much as the quality of the work. Artists often produce a number of versions of the same work, with minor variations, at high speed for the tourist trade. There are younger, more innovative painters whose work is highly prized by overseas collectors, but their paintings are more often sold outside China than at home.

Reproductions

Wood-block colour reproductions of great classic and modern works can be found mainly in Beijing. These are by no means cheap, but they are the product of a great tradition of painstaking craft. An inexpensive alternative is to look for rubbings of the inscriptions and illustrations on memorial tablets. These are available in black-and-white or tinted and can be very striking.

Carpets

Carpets, mostly woollen and some silk, are hand-woven in many parts of China, with Beijing, Tianjin and the minority areas of the north-west (the wool-producing regions of Mongolia and Xinjiang, and Tibet) having the longest traditions. The designs on the minority nationality carpets are akin to those of Persia and Pakistan, while the Beijing carpets feature larger blocks of colour and more pictorial designs. Prices are lower than in Europe and North America, but shipping charges and customs duties may bring the prices up to overseas levels.

Jade

Jade carving has a history of several thousand years in China. The Chinese term for jade, *yu*, covers a variety of stones, principally jadeite and nephrite. These are rare in China, and much of the jade carved in China comes from the Canadian west coast. Jade is prized for its hardness, lustre and clarity, all qualities associated with human virtue. The hardness of the stone makes carving arduous: in the past, a single piece might take an artisan years to complete, and even with today's power tools, it is a slow process. To create the finest pieces, skilled carvers envisage a form particularly suited to the colour, shape and texture of the piece of jade before them. These days, however, jade carving for the tourist market is all too often the laborious mass production of standard designs.

Ivory Ivory can be elegant and ornate – a favorite with collectors is the set of concentric balls carved from a single piece of ivory. Here, as with jade, the antique pieces tend to be the more original, while the modern, more mass-produced ones are often just a waste of a dwindling resource.

The ivory pieces sold in China are carved from African elephant tusks. The African elephant is now recognized by the Convention on International Trade in Endangered Species (CITES) as an endangered animal. Countries which are CITES signatories may forbid importation of ivory without an appropriate licence. If you have any intention of buying ivory, you should check current customs regulations at home before leaving for China.

Lacquer Lacquerware is created by painting numerous layers of the purified and tinted resin of the lac tree onto a base of wood, leather or copper. The result is a durable and shiny surface in red or black, or a combination of the two, typically on vases, plates and trays. Alternatively, vessels are thickly coated with over a hundred layers of the mat red cinnabar lacquer, which is then carved in intricate patterns of relief. Lacquer is very good value – a few pounds or dollars will buy a black tray with calligraphic or representational designs in red, or a small carved lacquer box. Workshops producing lacquerware are not usually included on foreign visitors' itineraries, since the material and its vapours can cause irritation.

Cloisonné *Cloisonné* is an ornamental enamelware made by dividing the surface of a copper vessel (vase, pendant, ashtray, animal shape etc.) into tiny segments (French *cloisons*) with copper wire. These sections are filled with enamel glazes of different colours, then fired and polished. Beijing is celebrated for its blue and turquoise *cloisonné*, but red, yellow, pink, white and black are effectively used in creating floral and geometric patterns. The making of *cloisonné* is technically demanding, and many of the pieces offered for sale are flawed. Care is advised in making selections, for quality as well as design.

Chops

Chops are pieces of soft stone, often carved, with a flat base, into which letters or characters can be incised. The chop is dipped into a red ink paste and pressed on to a sheet of paper. Chops are often used in China like an official stamp or signature, and are an elegant adornment to a letter or book. If you plan to have a personal chop made, it is an idea to ask a Chinese acquaintance to give you a Chinese name, since characters look better and more authentic for a chop than Western letters. The cost of a chop depends mostly on the size and quality of the stone you choose. You will then pay an amount per character or letter for carving. Carvers, who can be found wherever tourists go, either at government shops or as street-vendors, will often do the carving by the next day. The more skilled can offer a variety of calligraphic styles, from straightforward printed characters to the ornate and archaic oracle-bone style. If the carver does not supply ink, buy it before going home: chop-ink costs pennies for a lifetime supply (one small tin) and is hard to find outside China.

Other handicrafts

Other distinctively Chinese and quite inexpensive handicrafts include paper-cuts, dough-dolls, kites, clay figures and bamboo-ware. It is well worth looking for regional variations in whichever crafts interest you, and inquiring about local crafts, as you travel through China.

Getting it home

Large items like carpets can usually be shipped by the store that sells them, and this is the best plan if you are not intending to use them in China. Hotels and Friendship Stores will mail parcels, and major branches of New China Bookstore will mail books bought there.

Foreign residents leaving China can have crates made up and shipped. This can be done through their place of work or at Friendship Stores. Chinese customs may often demand that the crates be opened, unpacked, inspected and repacked, which can make departure even more eventful and memorable than it might otherwise be. Insure goods where possible, as things can get broken and a claim made against the shippers from outside China is unlikely to get results.

The land and the people

The third largest country in the world (after the Soviet Union and Canada), China is a land of great geographic diversity. Within its borders can be found the world's highest mountain and lowest depression, along with arid deserts, tropical jungles, high plateaux, broad rolling prairies and fertile river valleys. The China that most foreigners see is largely composed of densely populated cities and farming communities.

Climate Climatic variation is as wide as geographic. The north-western and western half of the country is a dry land

Temperature and precipitation chart
Seasonal values are given for the most visited cities of Beijing, Shanghai and Guangzhou, plus the north-western city of Xi'an, and Chengdu in the south-west. Average daily temperatures are in degrees Celsius, and monthly precipitation is in millimetres.

City		January	April	July	October
Beijing:	temperature	4	13	25	13
	precipitation	3	22	197	21
Shanghai:	temperature	3	14	28	18
	precipitation	44	111	143	47
Guangzhou:	temperature	14	22	29	24
	precipitation	39	159	220	52
Xi'an:	temperature	1	14	27	13
	precipitation	8	62	106	62
Chengdu:	temperature	6	17	26	17
	precipitation	5	51	229	48

of deserts and mountains. Rainfall is uncertain, and temperature variations between summer and winter are extreme. In contrast, in the south-east, conditions are semi-tropical, with less temperature variation and abundant rainfall (to a soggy high of over 2 m – 6 feet – a year in some places).

The best times of year to travel in China are spring (April–May) and autumn (September–October). In these months, rainfall is low, daytime temperatures are mild, and nights are cool. In winter, it is cold but dry in the north, while the damper south can also seem very cold. Summers are hot and wet in most of the areas travellers visit. In eastern and central China the sauna-like humidity of the 'yellow plum' season of late May and early June is followed by typhoons and downpours, which also hit the south, in July and August.

Rivers

Three major river systems drain almost half of China's territory and sustain most of its 1.2 thousand million people.

Yangtze

The greatest of these is the Yangtze, or *Changjiang* (long river), as it is known in Chinese. The Yangtze, the third longest river in the world, has its headwaters high in the mountains between Tibet and Qinghai province and empties into the East China Sea at Shanghai. As it crosses the East China Plain, the Yangtze marks a psychological division in China between north and south, which is manifested in one way that can be clearly observed on crossing the river – houses to the north of the river have chimneys, while those to the south do not. A government fuel-conservation policy permits only residents of north China to heat their homes. (There is heating in hotels and buildings used by foreigners, however.)

Yellow

The Yellow River, China's second longest river, also has its headwaters in Qinghai. As it flows through the loess (loam) plains of north China it picks up yellowish sediment which it carries to its lower reaches, at the rate of 1.6 thousand million tons a year. The silt deposited on the river-bed has raised the level of the

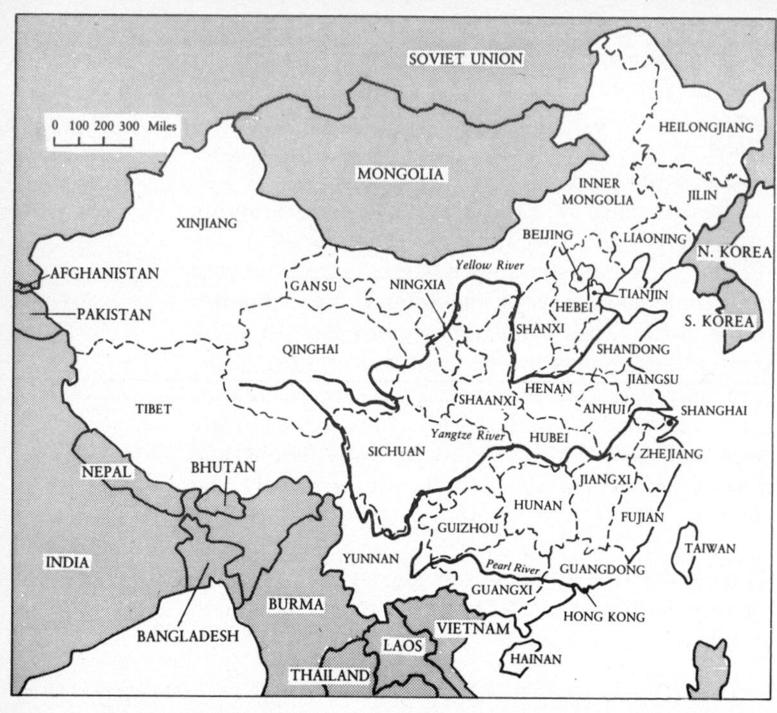

The People's Republic of China: rivers and administrative regions

river and extensive dikes have been necessary to contain its flow. In many places, the Yellow River flows at a level higher than the surrounding countryside. Over the centuries, the river has been known as 'China's Sorrow', since breaches in the dikes have led to sudden and catastrophic floods, unleashing devastation on communities along its banks.

Pearl The Pearl River is the longest river of south China. Its main tributary, the West River, originates in the mountains of Yunnan in China's south-west and, after being joined by the North and East Rivers, flows into the South China Sea at Guangzhou. The fertile delta of the Pearl provides much of the food for Guangdong province and Hong Kong.

Centres of population The great bulk of China's population lives in east and south China, with the highest concentrations being

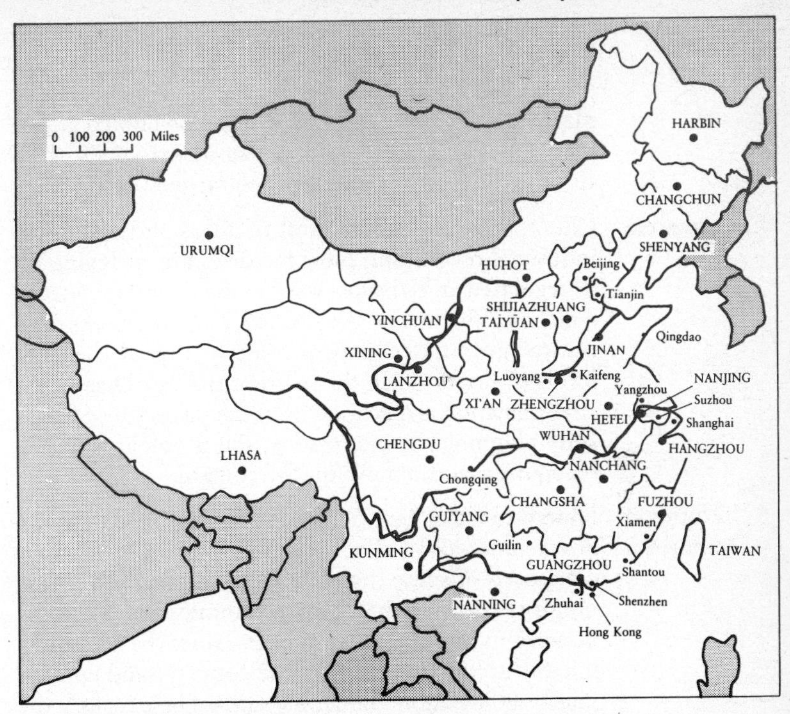

The People's Republic of China: provincial capitals and other major cities

along the Yangtze River and the eastern seaboard. These areas have most of the good arable land that comprises only about 12 per cent of China's territory.

China's most populous cities are found here. The largest urban areas include Beijing (population 9 million, and rising fast) and the nearby metropolis of Tianjin (8 million) in the north, Shanghai (12 million) in east-central China and Guangzhou (5 million) in the south. Inland and to the west along the Yangtze River lie the industrial city of Wuhan (4 million) and Chongqing (7 million), the largest city in the most populous province, Sichuan.

Rural areas

Eighty per cent of the population still lives outside the cities, in the farming counties and villages of rural China. Until the last few years, the Chinese authorities largely avoided the mass migration to the cities seen in so many third-world countries. This was achieved first by a strict policy of household registration, and then by government initiatives allowing the peasantry greater prosperity. Recently, however, the increased pressure placed by a growing rural population on limited arable land has led several million peasants to seek their fortunes in the cities, notably Beijing and Guangzhou.

Environment

China, and rural China most of all, is undergoing an industrial revolution. New factories are springing up unregulated and unsupervised in the countryside, and emitting effluent into the country's air and rivers. The central government has become aware of the high levels of pollution in the major cities, and has made environmental protection one of the priorities of future state planning. In the regions, the problem is barely recognized and almost out of control.

National minorities

Ninety-four per cent of China's citizens belong to the Han nationality. The remaining six per cent is composed of some fifty-five ethnic minorities. These minority peoples have an economic and strategic importance beyond their numbers, since the areas they inhabit occupy over half of the country, and contain much of the nation's mineral wealth. These include the huge 'autonomous zones' of Tibet, Xinjiang and Mongolia in west and north China, which border on countries with which relations have been uneasy in the recent past. The central government in Beijing attempts to accommodate its minorities by offering symbolic autonomy and permitting some cultural identity.

In general, the Han place great emphasis on conforming to their norms and view with amusement, condescension or even hostility those who do not share their customs. Where the distribution of population of the minority peoples is more scattered, as is the case with the Hui (Chinese Muslims) and Manchurians, or when they are found in smaller numbers, like the tribes of the tropical south-west, relations between the Han and minority peoples are generally peaceable. However, relations are often uneasy with those ethnic groups which remain less assimilated and retain their own language, religion and traditions. To control the Mongolians, the Uighurs of Xinjiang, and especially the Tibetans, large numbers of officials and soldiers of the Han nationality have been settled in the minority regions. This policy has as often increased as reduced racial tensions. In Tibet, demonstrations in favour of greater religious, cultural or political autonomy have been brutally suppressed by the Chinese authorities.

Population control

After a century of turmoil in which China's population remained at around 400 million, the stability promised by the establishment of the People's Republic, combined with Mao Zedong's idea that China's greatest strength lay in its numbers, sparked a population explosion. By the 1982 census there were over a thousand million Chinese, with the babyboomers of the 1950s ready to start their own families. The strain placed on the country's resources by its burgeoning population is viewed as a threat to modernization.

Since the early 1980s, the government has imposed a 'one-child' policy on all couples (national minorities are exempted). The policy has proved to be fairly effective in curbing the rise of population in overcrowded cities. It has also given rise to a generation of 'little emperors', the indulged and often wilful single children of urban families. The one-child rule has been much harder to enforce in the countryside where families still average just under three children. China's peasants have always wanted many sons to carry on the family line, work the land and care for them in their old age (daughters marry into other households and take care of their parents-in-law). New policies reintroducing farming based on the family unit have effectively encouraged larger families, with the increased labour-power they bring, while the lack of welfare programmes for the elderly in the villages mean that peasants still need children to rely on as they grow older. Indications that the one-child policy was failing have led to heavier penalties for those who bear more children, but many peasants are willing to pay whatever fines are imposed in their quest for male offspring.

Identity

Native place

A sense of one's native place is an important part of the Chinese identity. People are aware of where their ancestors came from, and will call that place home even if they have never visited it themselves. For example, in the early part of this century, many of the inhabitants of the port city of Ningbo drifted into the growing metropolis of Shanghai in search of work, and their descendants still call themselves 'Ningbo people', even though many have never been to Ningbo. Respect for the ancestral home is also the reason that many overseas Chinese continue to support the communities from which their ancestors fled poverty or oppression to live in Hong Kong or the West.

Unit In rural China, the major organizational structure in an individual's life is the village. The equivalent organization in the city is the unit. Generally the place of work, the unit is the source of housing, medical care, pensions, tickets to cultural or sporting events, permission to marry and have children, training and opportunities to study abroad, as well as income.

It is difficult to leave one unit for a better job in another. Units have the right to refuse to release their employees, and so elaborate and costly negotiations are often required before a transfer can take place. With the new economic policies, greater mobility between jobs, and therefore between units, is slowly becoming accepted. Greater flexibility allows hope for those assigned to work unsuited to their aptitude and abilities, but also endangers the less capable employees who were protected by the 'iron rice-bowl' of guaranteed employment.

Women The Confucian society of traditional China was male dominated, and the Communist Party has moved more slowly than many had hoped in the direction of equality of the sexes. While many women have moved into non-traditional jobs in the last forty years, some of these may be threatened by a government move to resolve youth unemployment by encouraging women to withdraw from the labour force to look after their children and households. The overwhelming majority of China's leaders are men, but women have held some positions of power, serving for example as head of the Bank of China, Textile Minister and the governor of a province.

There is, officially at least, no 'women's movement' of the kind that exists in the West. The officially sponsored

Women's Federation concerns itself with matters such as birth–control education and attempting to improve childcare and working conditions for women. There are, however, some women among the urban 'intellectual class' who are calling into question the traditional role they are still expected to play in society; one of them is the writer Zhang Jie, whose stories depict women in roles other than those of the conventional wife and mother.

Marriage

Marriages are often still arranged, particularly in the countryside. However, the system works rather differently from the way it did before 1949. Many couples are still introduced by go-betweens, but they can decide for themselves whether or not to marry, rather than meeting for the first time at the ceremony. In the cities, the difficulties many people encounter in meeting suitable partners are often overcome by marriage bureaux, the match-making efforts of friends or dance-parties arranged by their units.

China is not a country with a tradition of casual relationships between men and women. If a couple are going out together, the assumption is that they will marry, and they risk the disapproval of family and friends if they fail to do so.

As part of the policy to limit population growth, the government encourages late marriage. In the cities the standard ages for marrying are 26–9 for men and 24–6 for women; in the countryside, the ages are a few years younger. In order to marry it is necessary for people to receive approval from their units, and then to register their marriage with the civil authorities. Weddings are celebrated with as lavish a banquet as the couple can afford. On the day of the celebration, the bride and groom wear all new clothes, each with a large paper flower, red for celebration, pinned to their jackets. In the cities, newlyweds often like to have photographs taken in rented Western-style wedding attire. Weddings are more traditional in the countryside, though the sedan chairs that once carried the bride to her new husband and home have now given way to trucks, tractors or bicycles.

Gifts are provided by the groom to the bride's family to compensate for their loss. As consumer expectations rise, the cost of a young man getting married often takes the resources of the whole family for several years. Younger sons may have a long wait ahead unless they can find a woman whose family has modest expectations.

Divorce Divorce has been legal in China since the passing of the marriage law in the early 1950s. However, divorce is still not a preferred solution. Great efforts are made on the part of work units, neighbourhood committees and legal workers to mediate marital problems. When attempts at compromise fail, divorce is granted, but it carries a stigma – particularly for women, who seldom remarry.

Death In cities, the dead are cremated, but traditional burial practices are returning to rural China. Burial mounds can be seen from the windows of trains and buses while travelling in the countryside. White is the colour of mourning, and wreaths are made of white paper flowers. Processions of mourners, some beating gongs and blowing horns, noisily escort the deceased to their final resting place. Black arm-bands are often worn by those in mourning for a relative.

A look at the past

For the ancient Chinese, the land they lived in was not a country, but the world, 'all under heaven' or 'all within the four seas'. Their emperors were 'sons of heaven', austere figures as awesome and distant as heaven itself. Emperors governed, it was believed, because heaven recognized their virtue and gave them power; when a ruler became corrupt, this 'mandate of heaven' was taken away and conferred on another.

Recording the rise and fall of dynasties and justifying transfers of power in terms of a 'mandate of heaven' has been the work of Chinese historians for over two thousand years. Each dynasty that has taken power in China has required that historians portray the final rulers of overthrown regimes as degenerate and unworthy of heaven's blessing, while the conquerors, by their virtue and strength, deserve the power and authority they seized on the battlefield. (Such manipulation of history is not unique to China, of course; Shakespeare did as much for the Tudors, by showing the last of the preceding Yorkists, Richard III, as a murderous tyrant. For the Chinese, though, this kind of historical revisionism was institutionalized, and repeated with each dynastic change.) The communist leadership in China, more than any of the imperial dynasties, has regularly rewritten both the distant and recent past to support present policies, to condemn purged leaders or to praise those who are to be rehabilitated.

Beginnings

China has the longest continuous civilization in the world. It was born in the fertile Yellow River valley of north China. Five sage emperors are said to have governed the region from about 3000 BC. These were followed, around 2000 BC, by Yu the Great, who showed his virtue by leading his subjects in controlling the floods that have always plagued the Yellow

Chinese history at a glance

Xia dynasty	21st–16th centuries BC
Shang dynasty	16th–12th centuries BC
Zhou dynasty	1122–256 BC
Qin dynasty	221–206 BC
Han dynasty	206 BC–AD 220
Period of division	220–581
Sui dynasty	581–618
Tang dynasty	618–907
Song dynasty	960–1279
Yuan (Mongol) dynasty	1279–1368
Ming dynasty	1368–1644
Qing (Manchu) dynasty	1644–1911
Republic of China	1911–49
People's Republic	1949–present

River region. History records Yu as the founder of the Xia dynasty.

Shang and Zhou

The Shang dynasty followed the Xia, ruling north China for most of the second millennium BC. The Shang was China's bronze age, and is survived by finely wrought and technically sophisticated ritual vessels unearthed from tombs and displayed in museums in China and throughout the world. The histories record that the Shang dynasty fell after a depraved and tyrannical emperor lost the 'mandate of heaven' and was defeated by the first ruler of the succeeding Zhou dynasty.

The Zhou (1122–256 BC) was the dynasty whose elaborate court ritual was commended by Confucius, an itinerant philosopher and teacher from the state of Lu (part of present-day Shandong province in north-east China). Confucius also taught that by imitating the virtuous deeds of past emperors, present rulers could achieve social harmony and the perpetuation of their own rule. As well as works on statecraft and divination (see Beliefs), Confucius is credited with compiling China's first collection of poetry, *The Book of Songs*.

A moon rising white
Is the beauty of my lovely one.
Ah, the tenderness, the grace!
Heart's pain consumes me.

A moon rising bright
Is the fairness of my lovely one.
Ah, the gentle softness!
Heart's pain wounds me.

A moon rising in splendour
Is the beauty of my lovely one.
Ah, the delicate yielding!
Heart's pain torments me.

(from *The Book of Songs*:
translation from Cyril Birch,
ed., *Anthology of
Chinese Literature*)

The great dynasties

Qin

From the chaos that followed the fall of the Zhou emerged the force that was to unite much of north and south China for the first time. During the short-lived Qin dynasty (221–209 BC) a series of walls built to protect China's northern frontiers from marauding tribesmen were extended to form the Great Wall, which still stretches from the China Sea to the Gobi Desert.

The mighty First Emperor of Qin rejected the Confucian ideal of rule by example. Instead he introduced a draconian rule of law, destroyed copies of Confucian books and ordered scholars buried alive. For these actions, he was vilified as a tyrant until Mao Zedong (who, by his own account, had many more scholars killed) expressed admiration for him. The First Emperor was buried outside his capital of Chang'an (present-day Xi'an) with a magnificent army of larger than life terracotta horses and soldiers. Many of these have been excavated, and are on view at the burial site.

Han The Han (206 BC–220 AD) was the first of the long-lived dynasties of the historical period. Han rulers professed to follow the teachings of Confucius, and governed their empire with an ordered bureaucracy. In the second century BC, the 'Martial Emperor' Wudi embarked on military adventures to the west, aimed at expanding the empire, subduing 'barbarian' tribes and capturing horses. Also in the reign of Wudi, the Great Historian Sima Qian, despite being obliged to castrate himself for defending a disgraced general, wrote his *Historical Records*, a comprehensive history of the world (that is, China) to that time.

The Han was an age of scientific and technological advance in farming, war, and the production of paper and fine textiles. Among the most celebrated objects recovered from the tombs of the rich and powerful are two suits made of jade squares stitched with gold and silver thread, which clothed the bodies of a prince and princess of the ruling house in their tomb in present-day Hebei province.

The fall of the Han marked the beginning of four centuries when China was again divided into regional warring states. The empire was briefly united under the Sui dynasty (581–618), which was itself overturned by the founders of the greatest of Chinese ruling houses, the Tang.

Tang The Tang (618–907), especially the reign of the 'Brilliant Emperor' Xuanzong in the middle of the eighth century, was the golden age of Chinese courtly and cultural life. The poets Li Bai and Du Fu, who flourished in this period, are still regarded as China's greatest.

Thoughts on a peaceful night

The moonlight shines before my bed,
White as frost upon the ground.
Towards the moon I lift my head
And dream that I am homeward bound.

(Li Bai, 701–62)

Han Gan, court artist to the Brilliant Emperor, is best known for his horse-paintings, some of which survive. The most familiar artifacts of the Tang are glazed figures of courtiers and concubines, horses and camels, which have been excavated at burial sites. The Tang was the most cosmopolitan period of Imperial China, with foreign goods coming into China through its ports and overland across the Silk Road, which led from Chang'an to the Mediterranean.

Buddhism, which had entered China in the first century AD and become widespread in the period of the warring states, received official sanction in the early Tang, when the Chinese monk Xuanzang (also known as Tripitaka) was sent to India to collect scriptures. Legends tell that he was accompanied on his mission by the monkey king Sun Wukong, and their miraculous adventures are immortalized in the sixteenth-century novel *Journey to the West* (or *Monkey*).

Song

China under the Song dynasty (960–1279) was an increasingly secular and prosperous society, with great and wealthy cities. The diversity of city life is captured on a long horizontal scroll painting entitled 'Qingming (Clear and Bright) Festival by the River'. With an eye for minute detail reminiscent of Breughel, the artist Zhang Zeduan shows camel trains, ox-carts and sedan chairs, merchants, tradesmen and labourers thronging the streets of the Song capital of Kaifeng. Copies of this painting can be seen at many centres, including the Palace Museum in Beijing and the Shanghai Museum.

During the Song, there was a revival of the art of calligraphy, and great technological advances were made in porcelain production and printing. A reinterpreted Confucianism became the basis of a nationwide system of examinations held to staff the bureaucracy. Following a defeat by the Mongols in the north, the Song retreated south and established a new capital at Hangzhou, a city described by the Venetian Marco Polo in the late thirteenth century as 'without doubt the finest and most splendid city in the world'.

Yuan The nomadic Mongols, descendants of Genghis Khan, established themselves as the Yuan dynasty (1279–1368), and largely adopted Chinese patterns of rulership. The Yuan emperors moved the capital to Beijing, where they designed the Imperial Palaces that now occupy the centre of that city.

Ming The growth of cities and the rise of a commercial class that had begun in the Song continued into the Ming (1368–1644), the last Han Chinese dynasty. Blue and white porcelain, for which the Ming dynasty is celebrated, was poured onto world markets by an expanding empire. Under the Ming, power was concentrated as never before in the hands of the emperor, whose edicts were carried out by an increasingly large scholar-bureaucracy. The Ming ruling house played out the traditional pattern of dynastic rise and fall, both in its austere beginnings and in its final degeneration. In 1644 an effete monarch, surrounded by palace eunuchs and concubines and kept in a state of ignorance as his empire collapsed around him, finally hanged himself on the hill behind the Imperial Palace while the armies of a peasant brigand entered Beijing.

Thirteen Ming emperors are buried in a valley 49 kilometres (30 miles) outside Beijing. Two tombs have been excavated and refurbished, while the remaining eleven are in varying stages of gracious dereliction. The 'Sacred Way' that leads into the valley is guarded by mighty statues of officials and animals.

Qing The emperors of the Qing (1644–1911), members of the northern Manchu race, presided over the last flourishing of imperial China, its contact with Western powers, and its final collapse. 'Our celestial empire possesses all things in prolific abundance', the Emperor Qianlong told King George III's ambassador in 1793, but the foundations of that empire were crumbling. The fall of a noble family through overspending and corruption, which is portrayed in the great Qing novel *The Story of the Stone* (or *The Dream of the Red Chamber*), is often said to represent the decline of the empire itself. Economically and morally undermined by the opium trade with Britain, the Qing empire was humiliated by defeat in the Opium Wars of the 1840s.

In the 1850s the country was ravaged by the Taiping Rebellion, a combination of peasant uprising and quasi-Christian holy war which left twenty million people dead before it was suppressed. Further defeats followed at the hands of foreign powers, including the Japanese in the 1890s. There were more rebellions as well, the most infamous being that of the xenophobic Boxers at the turn of the century. In their final years in power, the Qing rulers tried desperately to strengthen China by adopting Western technology while preserving traditional Confucian moral order. Their attempts came too late to prevent the overthrow of the imperial house in the Republican Revolution of 1911.

The physical remains of the Qing dynasty reflect the Manchu rulers' fascination with the exotic West. The old Summer Palace, built in the 1740s and sacked by British troops in 1860, was Italian rococo; its replacement, now one of Beijing's most popular tourist spots, combines the best and the worst of the Qing aesthetic. Beautifully landscaped around an artificial lake, with elegant bridges and walkways, it has halls and palaces stuffed with treasures over-ornamented in a style reminiscent of the contemporary Victorian age in Britain. Most bizarre is the stone replica of an American paddle-steamer built at vast expense with money raised to modernize the navy.

Republic

The Republican period (1911–49) was a time of political and military turmoil. Sun Yat-sen, instigator of the revolution and first president of the Republic, could not hold together the disparate factions that had brought down the empire, and the country became divided amongst competing warlords. Internationally China fared little better. China had entered the First World War on the side of the victorious allies, but when the combatants gathered in 1919 to conclude a final treaty at Versailles, Chinese territories formerly held by Germany were awarded to Japan rather than returned to China. Feelings of national humiliation gave rise to an assertion of nationalism, expressed in student-led demonstrations in Beijing on 4 May 1919.

The quest for a new national identity was part of a ferment of ideas, often called the May Fourth movement, that developed in the political chaos of the Republican period. It was a time of artistic innovation, as China's intellectuals confronted the modern world from the ruins of traditional China. Modern China's first great writer, Lu Xun, portrayed an old society hopelessly corrupt and in need of revolutionary change. Other writers and artists joined him in attacking the Chinese tradition with Chinese works bearing the mark of studies in the West and Japan.

> Thousands of dark, gaunt faces perish amid
>   the thorns,
> But who dares to shake the earth with wailing?
> My brooding thoughts roam the vast universe,
> When all sounds are hushed I hear the roar
>   of thunder!
>
> (Lu Xun, 1881–1936)

The great city of Shanghai, a small fishing-village in the 1850s, prospered in the Republican period as a Western-controlled enclave, its European monumental and domestic architecture a legacy of colonialism.

Among the many new social and political ideologies that flooded into China was communism, which gained a following in China after the Russian Revolution of 1917. From humble beginnings in 1921, and after a protracted civil war interrupted by Japanese occupation during the Second World War, the Chinese Communist Party (CP) and its Red Army overthrew the US-backed nationalist government of Chiang Kai-shek, which withdrew to the island of Taiwan. From the reviewing stand on the Gate of Heavenly Peace in the Imperial Palace in Beijing, CP Chairman Mao Zedong proclaimed the establishment of the People's Republic of China on 1 October 1949.

Snow (extract)
So rich in beauty is this great land
That countless heroes bowed the knee in awe.
The first Emperor of Qin and the Martial
Emperor of Han
Were lacking in literary grace,
The founders of Tang and Song
Had little poetry in their souls.
Even Genghis Khan,
Mighty son of heaven as he was,
Knew only how to shoot down eagles with
his bow.
All are past and gone!
For men of true greatness
Look to this age alone.

(Mao Zedong, 1893–1976)

People's Republic

The process of turning China into a modern socialist state has been fraught with drastic shifts in policy, reflecting both differences in personality and approach among the leaders who brought the communists to power, and the difficulties in transforming an ancient nation with a vast population.

The communists inherited a country divided and impoverished by a century of war and disruption, and their first task was to eliminate domestic opposition and secure their hold on power. Among their first moves were the dispossession of rural landlords and the distribution of land among the peasants. Factories and businesses were nationalized, and an alliance with Stalin's Russia brought Soviet technology and advisers to China. Thought-reform campaigns were initiated to prepare the Chinese people to build socialism.

In the mid-1950s, the Communist Party attempted, in the Hundred Flowers movement, to enlist the support of the nation's intellectuals by encouraging them to voice criticisms of the Party's performance. When the criticisms proved harsher than expected, many of those intellectuals found themselves condemned and imprisoned in the subsequent Anti-rightist campaign.

Disgruntled with the intellectuals and alienated from the post-Stalin Soviet Union, Mao Zedong launched the Great Leap Forward in 1958. It was an attempt to catapult China into a communist utopia through the sheer physical efforts of its workers and peasants. Village collectives were organized into people's communes, backyard furnaces were built in a misguided bid to boost steel production, and the populace was exhausted by a series of massive public-works projects. The failure of the Great Leap and a break with the Soviet Union combined with disastrous harvests to cause widespread famine as China entered the 1960s.

As the nation recovered from the Great Leap, China's leadership was deeply divided over the appropriate course for future development. One group of 'pragmatists' favoured more liberal economic policies, including a measure of private enterprise, in order to develop the economic base. This view was anathema to the 'ideologues' led by Mao Zedong, who feared that such policies would lead to a return of the capitalist system they had always opposed. By the mid-1960s, it seemed that the 'pragmatists' had gained the upper hand; Mao's response was the Cultural Revolution, which was both a counter-attack on his rivals in the leadership and an assault on the traditional culture which he felt was stifling the realization of his vision of Chinese socialism.

The Cultural Revolution (1966–76) began with a period of intense and violent conflict, and continued in a series of disruptive mass campaigns attacking those believed to be hostile to Mao and his radical ideology. Work-units were often told how many 'class enemies' they were expected to denounce in any given campaign, and this quota system inevitably led to betrayal, suspicion and injustice. Popular feeling against Mao, his wife Jiang Qing and their associates was demonstrated in riots which followed public mourning for state premier Zhou Enlai in the centre of Beijing on 5 April 1976. A coup following Mao's funeral later that year ended the 'ideologues'' hopes for taking power.

'Spoiling the view' by Hua Junwu

Following Mao's death, his Great Leap Forward and Cultural Revolution were denounced as disasters, wasting human and economic resources and damaging the fabric of Chinese society. After 1978 the pragmatists, led by the twice-purged Deng Xiaoping, took command. They stimulated the economy by encouraging entrepreneurship, dismantling agricultural collectives in favour of family farming, and permitting economic contact with the West.

The changes that Deng's reforms brought to China are visible everywhere. In Beijing, modern international hotels and office towers dominate the skyline, looking down on the Imperial Palaces and the Soviet-style public buildings of the Great Leap Forward. Throughout the country, hoardings advertising all manner of domestic and imported consumer products

The answer (extract)
I come into this world
Bringing only paper, a rope, a shadow,
To proclaim before the judgement
The voices of the judged:

Let me tell you, world,
I–do–not–believe!
If a thousand challengers lie beneath your feet,
Count me as number one thousand and one.

I don't believe the sky is blue;
I don't believe in the sound of thunder;
I don't believe that dreams are false;
I don't believe that death has no revenge.

(Bei Dao, b. 1949, translated by Bonnie S. McDougall)

have replaced the white-on-red Mao slogans of the 1960s and 1970s.

China's artists did their best to absorb and react to the thousands of years of their own culture and hundreds of years of Western culture that had suddenly become available to them. In the arts, the doctrinaire socialist realism of the first three decades of the People's Republic was replaced by more questioning works in a number of different styles from neo-classical to dada. Writers whose work set the tone for the 1980s included the novelist Wang Meng, who experimented with a Chinese version of 'stream of consciousness' writing, and the symbolist poet Bei Dao.

Economic liberalization and Western influence transformed Chinese society in the 1980s. However, the CP leadership showed itself unwilling to accept the social and cultural changes brought about by its economic initiatives. Media attacks on 'spiritual pollution' and 'bourgeois liberalism' became more common as the decade advanced. China's economy expanded rapidly but unevenly in the 1980s, fuelling an inflation unknown since the 40s. Discontent with the economy and disillusionment with the increasingly autocratic rule of the elderly leaders of the CP led to student demonstrations in many cities, culminating in the mass protests of the democratic movement in the capital during the months of April and May 1989. As in the May Fourth protests seventy years earlier, student protestors were joined by other young people, intellectuals and the working population of Beijing. Unable to agree on an appropriate course of action, a divided CP leadership delayed for several weeks. Then, furious at the demonstrators' defiance, and humiliated in front of visiting Soviet leader Mikhail Gorbachev, Deng and his elderly colleagues crushed the protests with tanks and machine guns on the night of 3–4 June 1989. The student leaders were killed, imprisoned or forced to flee abroad. In the ensuing repression, the leadership has shown itself at a loss for ideas and at odds with its own people, forced to rely on discredited Maoist slogans and the might of the army to stay in power.

> Resigned to springs by tyranny defiled,
> Hair streaked with grey, I flee
> with wife and child.
> My dreams are haunted by a mother's
> tears.
> Atop the walls the victors' flag appears.
> I grieve for comrades lost, now
> ghosts forlorn,
> And seek with rhymes to face
> the daggers drawn.
> My poem made, I cannot write it
> down,
> The moonlight ripples on my
> dark silk gown.
>
> (Lu Xun, 1931)

Beliefs

The Chinese are adept at accommodating apparently mutually exclusive ideologies. As well as the traditional 'three teachings' of Confucianism, Daoism and Buddhism, the imported doctrines of Marxism, Christianity and entrepreneurial capitalism also exert an influence on society. The interaction of these systems of belief, whether within an individual or in society, produces complex behavioural patterns which the outside observer might find puzzling and inconsistent. Any attempt to understand the forces which influence behaviour in China must begin with a look back at the Chinese philosophical tradition.

Yin, yang and _dao_

In the Chinese tradition, there is no supreme being or creator. There is a myth which describes how the supernatural being Pan Gu created the earth, but this is a late (post-Han) and rather lame addition to the Chinese canon. According to more ancient beliefs, primordial chaos was transformed into order through the continuous interaction of the cosmic forces of *yin* and *yang*. *Yin*, the female principle, is represented in darkness, night, moisture and the moon; *yang*, the male principle, is found in their opposites: light, day, dryness and the sun. The harmonious interaction of these opposing but complementary forces results in the pattern of life known as *dao*, the way.

Confucianism

The Chinese social order and the moral justification for government in imperial China were based on ideas attributed to Confucius (551–479 BC). In an ideal Confucian society, order is maintained by ensuring that all people know their places in society and act appropriately. Confucius defined relationships of apparent mutual responsibility, but actual dominance and subservience, between ruler and subject, father and son, elder and younger brother and husband and wife. Books attributed to Confucius, though probably compiled after his death, include his *Analects* or sayings, *The Book of Songs* and the manual of divination called *The Book of Changes* (also known in the West as the *I Ching*). This last book has been used for over two thousand years as a guide to human action: the reader throws three coins, and the way they fall directs him or her to an oracular passage which, when correctly interpreted, indicates an appropriate course of action.

Confucianism has been a conservative influence on the Chinese throughout their history, insisting on the primacy of the past over the present, and the old over the young. It has been particularly oppressive towards women, whose position demanded obedience first to father, then to husband and finally to son. The importance Confucianism places on maintaining outward composure also forces people to suppress their feelings, which can cause enormous emotional stress. In the twentieth century Confucianism has come under attack, notably in the May Fourth period (1917–27), and in a mass campaign launched by the CP in the early 1970s. Despite the criticisms, the Chinese retain many of the values associated with Confucianism, most notably the respect of children for their parents, or 'filial piety'. China's leadership stands to gain from perpetuating a doctrine which aims at keeping society orderly; however, official pronouncements tend to advocate 'traditional morality' rather than referring explicitly to Confucianism.

Daoism

Daoism (also written 'Taoism' in many English-language books) rejects the constraints that define Confucianism. Where Confucianism is hierarchical and emphasizes responsibility, Daoism stresses spontaneity and the need to be at one with nature (the natural world and one's natural self). Though apparently contradictory, Confucianism and Daoism have complemented each other in the Chinese tradition, appealing to different sides of a person's character. Mandarins of the past might have been model Confucians in their official dealings, but they could still have adopted a Daoist approach to private life.

The supposed founder of Daoism was Laozi, a name which means simply 'old master'. Laozi is said to have been a contemporary of Confucius, but nothing is known of his life. He is survived only by a book of epigrams called *The Way and the Power*. Laozi regarded civilization and learning as the enemies of nature. The ideal man was an 'uncut block' (similar to the Western romantic ideal of the 'noble savage') and ideal behaviour consisted of non-intervention with the natural functioning of the world.

The greatest of Laozi's successors, Zhuangzi (fourth century BC) left a humorous and anecdotal text that bears his name. In it, freedom and integrity are qualities to be prized, and the pursuit of power is disdained.

The Daoist approach to power: avoid it!
(from *Zhuangzi*)
Zhuangzi was out fishing when two emissaries of the King of Chu came up to him and said: 'Our master wishes to entrust you with his realm.' Without putting down his rod or looking around, Zhuangzi said: 'I hear that in the king's palace there is a turtle which has been dead three thousand years, which the king has decorated and stores in a shrine. Do you think that turtle would prefer to be dead and honoured or alive and dragging its tail in the mud?' The messengers replied: 'It would rather be in the mud.' 'Go away', said Zhuangzi, 'and let me drag my tail in the mud.'

Philosophical and popular Daoism

Daoism began as a refined and quietist philosophy. Over the centuries, however, it has blended with other folk beliefs and practices to form an elaborate popular religion with many sects and, to quote one scholar, with an 'innumerable rabble' of gods and spirits. Popular Daoism as it is practised in Chinese villages involves ritual offerings to ancestors and household gods, and a cottage industry of shamans and geomancers. Like other aspects of the Chinese tradition, popular religion, frowned upon in the first thirty years of communist rule, underwent a revival in the years following the death of Mao.

Buddhism

Though it originated in India, and took hold in China in the chaos that followed the fall of the Han dynasty in the third century AD, Buddhism is regarded, with Confucianism and Daoism, as one of the fundamental 'three teachings' of ancient China. Up to the late Tang, Buddhism was sanctioned by Chinese rulers, who sponsored the carving of sculptures and encouraged the translation of scriptures, before turning against the religion in the middle of the ninth century. It has long held a strong influence on popular imagination, which can be seen today in the processions of the faithful to pray and offer incense at shrines and temples.

Buddhism teaches that life is painful, but that pain and sorrow may be eliminated by suppression of the self through meditation or performance of rituals. The believer attempts to achieve enlightenment and attain nirvana, an escape from the world.

The systems of belief outlined above have combined to produce patterns of behaviour that can be seen in Chinese communities everywhere. Confucianism has had the most obvious effect – its powerful sense of family loyalty and respect for elders has been a force for holding Chinese society together, and less positively, for suppressing the initiatives of the young. Daoism's influence has been more on private than public life, but a Daoist posture of disdain for worldly affairs is commonly expressed by many Chinese intellectuals. Buddhist influence can also be seen in the fatalism of the Chinese people, the peasantry most of all, in enduring centuries of natural disaster and tyranny with little active resistance.

Christianity

Christianity has been in China since at least the sixteenth century. The brilliant Jesuit emissary Matteo Ricci (1552–1610) won the respect of the Ming court for both his demonstrations of Western technology and the speed with which he acquired the education, manner and appearance of a Confucian official. Catholics like Ricci allowed themselves to become assimilated with the official class and permitted their converts to combine Catholicism with traditional beliefs in the time-honoured Chinese manner. Protestants, who were part of the nineteenth century military, economic and ideological invasion from the West, concentrated their efforts on the common people and were less tolerant of traditional beliefs and practices.

Both Catholics and Protestants were attacked in the anti-foreign fervour of the late Qing, and many perished at the hands of the Boxers. Christianity gained official sanction under the Republic, a period in which the ruling Nationalist Party was led by the professed Methodist Chiang Kai-shek (though his espousal of the religion may have been due more to his need for Western military and economic support than to spiritual devotion).

Following the communist victory of 1949, links with outside churches were severed, and foreign missionaries were sent home. During the Cultural Revolution, churches were closed, religion outlawed and Christians persecuted. In the 1980s religious belief and practice were permitted (though believers were not supposed to convert others), and several million Chinese exercised their right to believe. Those who had maintained their faith in secret were joined by young people curious to know about beliefs and practices so long forbidden to them. There was a strong resurgence of Christianity, especially Catholicism. (The Chinese Catholic church still has no formal ties with the Vatican, and retains the Latin mass.) By 1987, over a thousand Catholic and Protestant churches had reopened, and services were very well-attended. Major churches in Beijing and Shanghai are – Beijing: Dongtang Catholic Cathedral, 74 Wangfujing Street and the Protestant Church, 21 Meizha Alley, Dongdan Street North; Shanghai: Xujiahui Catholic Cathedral, 158 Puxi Road and the Community Church of Shanghai, 53 Hengshan Road.

Renewed intolerance

The official spirit of religious tolerance had begun to wear thin even before the suppression of the democracy movement in 1989. The government became fearful that increased adherence to religion could increase resistance to Party control. In Tibet, in particular, popular demonstrations against Chinese rule were led by monks still loyal to the exiled Dalai Lama. Many of the protestors, and Buddhists elsewhere, have been arrested.

Official fears that China's Catholics would unite and seek closer links with the Vatican led the authorities to arrest a number of bishops, priests and laymen, accusing them of 'undermining social stability'. Though freedom of belief remains in the Chinese constitution, many Chinese are now more cautious about exercising that freedom publicly. While visitors to China need not fear that their own religious practice will get them into trouble, some discretion is advised in dealing with Chinese believers.

Socialism

China's communist leaders have been faced with the problem of incorporating the Western ideology of Marxism into a traditional Chinese society. In a series of articles written before the CP came to power, Mao Zedong was credited with combining Marxism with Chinese conditions, in what became known by the cumbersome title of 'Marxism-Leninism-Mao Zedong Thought' (the term 'Maoism' has never been used in China). An attempt was made to adapt many of the old patterns; for example, loyalty to family was to be redirected into loyalty to Party and state.

To instruct people on how to live as socialists, the CP launched a series of emulation campaigns in the 1950s and 1960s. China's citizens were presented with selfless socialist heroes as models for correct behaviour. The most durable of these has been the young soldier Lei Feng, whose apocryphal diary, published after his death in a 1962 accident, expressed his desire to be an 'unrusting screw' in the great revolutionary machine. Other state-sponsored heroes come and go, but Lei Feng, with his message of untiring work and loyalty to the CP, is still held up as a model for the young. His image is periodically updated to align him with current CP policies. In 1988, Lei Feng, who had always been portrayed as the selfless collectivist repeatedly giving away his savings to those in need, was revealed instead to have invested his money wisely and turned a profit in a manner suited to the more capitalistic style of the times. By 1990, newly 'discovered' documents restored Lei Feng to his former role as a rigorously orthodox Party man.

Assault on tradition

The Cultural Revolution of 1966–76 was a direct attack on Chinese tradition, brought about by Mao's frustration with the CP's failure to realize his vision of a Chinese socialist state. Mao effectively turned the Chinese people, especially the young, against their past, with a view to destroying all that had gone before so that a new order could replace it. Brutal attacks by children on their teachers, and on anyone tainted by bourgeois thinking, religion or foreign connections, were commonplace in the late 1960s. Families were torn apart as children denounced their parents, and wives and husbands repudiated and divorced partners who came under suspicion or attack. Colleagues attacked each other, both to settle personal scores and to save themselves from condemnation. The only way to survive in the atmosphere of mutual betrayal and suspicion was to maintain a public face that was enthusiastic about the achievements of socialism and the policies of the Communist Party, and either suppress private thoughts and emotions completely or share them only with trusted friends.

The Cultural Revolution is now condemned for its undermining of social relations. Many older Chinese, especially after being elbowed aside in the stampede to get on a crowded bus, blame the political upheaval for what they see as a decline in standards of morality and public discipline. It is certainly true that the exclusively Chinese experience of the Cultural Revolution has been a factor in changing Chinese society, but laments of social decline are not unique to China.

The Communist Party in the 1990s has an uphill struggle to restore public confidence in its philosophy and policies. Attempts to revive the prestige of the Party and the optimism of the early years of the People's Republic are regarded with cynicism or, at best, boredom, by many people.

Market socialism

A recent factor influencing Chinese behaviour has been the national experiment with entrepreneurial capitalism, or 'market socialism' as it is sometimes called. The economic liberalization of the 1980s renewed personal ambition and initiative, and created considerable wealth for the successful. It also led to rising consumer expectations and intense jealousy of the newly rich, at a time when inflation was reducing living standards for many. These new pressures combine with the abiding problems of overcrowding and shortage of goods and services to increase the stress of daily life.

Factions within the leadership of the Communist Party, like the leaders of the Qing government in the late nineteenth century, profess to believe that Western technology can be imported without the 'spiritual pollution' of Western ideas. They choose to blame many of the problems in contemporary society on the influx of ideas incompatible with the Chinese tradition, and have cited the apparently foreign vices of exploitation, corruption and tax evasion as the reason for closing down a number of private businesses.

It may be that in time the entrepreneurial values of the 1980s will blend with the rhetoric of Marxism as harmoniously as do the apparently opposing beliefs of the traditional 'three teachings', but there is no sign that this will happen soon.

Behaviour

Various codes of behaviour govern how people get things done without disrupting others more than they have to. A foreigner in China can often deal more straightforwardly with Chinese colleagues and acquaintances than Chinese people can with each other; nevertheless, situations will occur where knowledge of Chinese ways will save time, frustration and honour, and may result in a course of action which is both harmonious and effective.

Making connections

The major force in social relations is *guanxi*, 'connections'. It is similar to the Western idea of 'networking', but it has a more comprehensive role in people's lives. *Guanxi* is a system of reciprocal benefit and obligation which involves using other people's good connections to get what is needed, and being prepared to offer favours in return. Chinese people need *guanxi* to bypass cumbersome official channels for getting a better apartment or job, buying furniture, hiring a car or obtaining special medical treatment. For those without skills or services of use to the person whose help is being sought, money and gifts are the alternative. Jokes about the demanding of gifts became common in the early 1980s, as witness this pun: a supplicant is told by the official whose help he needs that *yanjiu* (research into the problem) is needed. *Yanjiu* pronounced with different tonal stress indicates the official's real need: cigarettes and alcohol (*yan* and *jiu*).

Guanxi pervades every aspect of Chinese life, enabling those with influence to 'go in by the back door' or circumvent usual channels, and placing those who are unwilling or unable to use it at a considerable disadvantage.

Saving face

'Face', the capacity to respect oneself in dealings with others, is of vital importance. To 'lose face', by being proved wrong or shown to be incompetent, is a humiliation. In dealing with others, it is necessary to allow them to 'save face', or maintain their prestige, even in cases where it is clear they are at fault; they should do as much for you if the positions were reversed.

While it is fine to be forceful and insistent in dealing with Chinese guides and officials, losing your temper involves a loss of face for all concerned and achieves nothing. In conflicts, resist the temptation to move in for the kill. Making an official look bad in front of his or her colleagues and superiors imposes a crushing blow. Since the same official will probably continue to be assigned to work with you, it is counterproductive to make him or her an enemy.

It should be borne in mind that it is often very difficult, for both cultural and practical reasons, for a Chinese person to admit responsibility for a mistake or accident. For example, a sales assistant clerk who admits to breaking some valuable object while handing it to a customer will be required to pay for it, something that would be impossible out of his or her wages. He or she will have no alternative but to blame the customer, and considerations of face make it impossible to back down.

Indirection

It may be impossible for a Chinese person to explain the real reason for an action or inaction. Instead, an alternative, and often implausible, reason may be provided. It is important not only to tolerate incomprehensible behaviour, but also, more importantly, to make an intelligent guess at the reasons behind it. Here are some examples:

when a book is taken off bookshop or library shelves for political reasons, a sales assistant will say it has 'sold out', and a librarian will say 'we don't have it any more.' They are closing the subject without having to raise the embarrassing question of why the book is not there.

the authors have heard a Chinese tour-guide in Shanghai telling a tourist that the Yuyuan Garden, one of the city's major attractions, had been torn down and that they would have to stick to their original plan of a factory visit. The garden was intact, and still is; the guide resorted to the fabrication rather than explain that he would be in trouble with the factory management had the expected tour-group failed to show up.

In such cases, a Westerner might react angrily to what he or she perceives as a lie. (The irritation may be compounded by the fact that Chinese people smile or even laugh to cover embarrassment.) Such a reaction is neither appropriate nor useful. The intention of the (often transparent) untruth is to signal that pressures prevent the satisfaction of the request, and that further discussion is pointless. A Chinese person would read the signal, and would probably drop the matter. A foreigner can sometimes, with intelligent guesswork and polite but persistent probing, find out the underlying problem and propose a solution.

Compromise The Chinese approach to problem-solving is often one of glossing over problems rather than dealing with issues. For reasons of face, disputes are often dealt with by mediating a compromise which allows both sides to feel vindicated. This approach can create enormous problems for Western businesspeople working in China who are used to functioning in the framework of international law. Legal decisions can be overruled in favour of political compromises, and a problem that might be cleared up with a couple of phone calls in the West may take weeks of painstaking and expensive negotiation in China.

Indifference Foreigners who live in China are often shocked by the way people ignore or even laugh at those who are in trouble. Passers-by seldom come to the assistance of those who are taken ill, injured or attacked in public places. It is a custom that distresses many Chinese as well; for example, many incidents in the stories of Lu Xun demonstrate his anger at the general indifference to, and relish at, the sufferings of others. This indifference stems both from the Confucian tradition of caring only for those with whom one has a familial or instrumental relationship, and from a long-standing aversion among private citizens to becoming involved with an unpredictable system of law enforcement.

Punctuality

In Asia, only the most powerful officials can show their authority by being late. The foreign visitor should attend meetings, outings and meals on time. It is very difficult for a low-level official or guide to arrange appointments with those of higher rank, or even to get a bus for an outing, and it is he or she who suffers in terms of face and *guanxi* if the foreigner is late or fails to show up.

Courtesies

First meetings are conducted on a much more formal level than, for example, their North American equivalents. Physical contact should be limited to a handshake, though a slight bow and a polite greeting will do just as well. Personal comments and remarks on physical appearance, especially of women, should be avoided. There are other matters, however, that crop up much earlier in conversation in China than outside. Do not be surprised to be asked your age, marital status and income by relative strangers. Such questions are standard conversational gambits in China and are not meant to be rude.

In discussion with foreigners, Chinese people may refer to China's relative backwardness. However, it is bad manners for foreigners to be overly critical of China (which is, after all, like insulting a host), or their own countries, of which they are considered representatives.

In China as elsewhere, people who feel awkward in an unfamiliar culture tend to make loud and disparaging remarks about the country and its people. Such remarks often reveal more about the speaker's inadequacies than the country's. This kind of behaviour is ill-mannered anywhere and China is no exception.

Terms of address

In Chinese, people are usually addressed by their surname and title. A factory manager called Qiao Guangpu (his surname is Qiao, his given name

Guangpu) is addressed as Qiao *changzhang*, 'Factory Manager Qiao'. The foreign visitor can use 'Mr' and 'Ms' (the Chinese terms are *xiansheng* and *nüshi* respectively), though they are seldom used by Chinese people. The once-common 'comrade' should not be used by foreigners, and is in fact used only on specific and limited occasions in Chinese society. Drivers, waiters and other service personnel can be addressed simply as *shifu*, a term meaning something like 'master-craftsman'.

It is common for Chinese friends, colleagues and classmates to address each other with the words *lao*, 'old', or *xiao*, 'little', before the surname. Thus Manager Qiao is *Lao* Qiao, 'Old Qiao', to his friends, and a girl student surnamed Li would be *Xiao* Li, 'Little Li', to her fellow-students. The visitor is advised to wait for a Chinese acquaintance to make the suggestion before changing to a more informal level of address.

Gift-giving and tipping

If you are making a gift to an institution, such as a university department or a government office, it should be presented at a public occasion, such as a banquet, so that as many people as possible will see it being given. This serves the dual purpose of maximizing appreciation and ensuring that the gift can be used by a number of people rather than being locked away in someone's office.

Gifts to an individual, however, should be made discreetly, since mutual surveillance is common among Chinese colleagues, and seeing others receive prized foreign commodities can give rise to jealousy. Appropriate souvenir-type gifts are postcards, notebooks and pens with the name of your country or home town on them. English speakers will appreciate books or cassette-tapes in English. Most Chinese people who deal regularly with foreigners own calculators, and many also have digital watches and Walkmans. Those who do not would like to.

Foreign cigarettes are a major currency of *guanxi*, and a useful key for opening back doors. China has a trillion-a-year cigarette habit, and foreign brands are highly prized and only sporadically available to

Chinese buyers. They are ideal tokens of appreciation for drivers, repairmen and commissionaires, and should be given as a gift at the beginning of a relationship rather than as a tip at the end. Cigarettes are a better gift for men than women.

Tipping is not yet a common practice. It is coming, though, and in this, as in other economic matters, Guangzhou is leading the way. Most guidebooks discourage tipping, and it is officially discouraged, but a case can be made for a tip to reward good service from guides and hotel workers. Most of them are relatively poorly paid, which accounts for the lack of enthusiasm many of them have for their jobs. A judicious tip might improve service. Some restaurants which serve foreigners now add a service charge to the bill, and in this case no further tip is required.

Friendship and favours

Friendships with Chinese people are enormously rewarding, both on a personal level, and for the insights they provide into Chinese individual and social life. Friendship with a foreigner can have advantages for a Chinese person as well, and favours are sometimes asked. Common requests made to foreign friends are to change RMB into FECs and to buy goods (such as cigarettes, tapes or medicines) at Friendship Stores or overseas. A more extreme request is for help getting someone into university in the West, something many established and upwardly mobile Chinese desire for themselves or their sons and daughters. It is often assumed that Westerners with good incomes will have sufficient pull to arrange entry into a university, accommodation, and even a scholarship. Such arrangements have been made in the past to cement business relationships and help friends. Sometimes these requests may come from virtual strangers. If you are not in a position to help, it is better to make this clear immediately, and thus avoid raising hopes unjustly.

Romance

Since the 1970s many happy and successful marriages have occurred between Chinese nationals and foreign teachers, students and others working and travelling in China. Few have gone smoothly from love to marriage, and most have encountered considerable bureaucratic obstruction before their final triumph. Getting married and moving to the West (which is what happens in almost every case) will require persistence and should not be undertaken lightly.

In recent years, some young Chinese who want to leave China have sought out potential Western marriage partners. Chinese women who do this are called 'international girls' or 'plane-ticket girls' by their peers, and are seldom popular. Marriages of convenience are common in China, but tend to appeal less to foreigners, who might do well to suspect sudden romantic advances from aspiring emigrants.

Casual affairs, especially between foreign men and Chinese women, can have disastrous effects, destroying marriage prospects and in extreme cases (such as those in which the foreigner is a diplomat or journalist) resulting in the Chinese partner being sent to a labour camp.

Chinese/foreign couples should behave with restraint in public. Even in these more liberated days affection between men and women is shown outside the home much less than in the West.

Physical contact in public is actually much more common among members of the same sex than between male–female couples. Holding hands and linking arms are signs of friendship and acceptance.

Crime Chinese cities are among the safest in the world, and an evening stroll, even for a single woman, presents hardly any risk. Crimes of violence are increasing, but are still infrequent by Western standards, and rarely involve foreigners. Penalties for crimes of violence are severe, and executions of those found guilty of murder, rape and even embezzlement are periodically publicized to remind citizens of the consequences of such actions.

Petty crime exists, and the same precautions should be taken as in any other country. There are pickpockets in crowds and on buses, and a foreign wallet is a good catch, though the penalty for being caught taking it is very high (several years of labour camp). Most theft from hotels is of hotel property rather than guests' property; still, money and small valuables should not be left out in hotel rooms or apartments where they present a temptation to cleaners and other staff. Some older hotels do not allow guests to keep their room keys, and people staying there should consider taking cash, passports and valuables such as cameras with them when they go out.

Officialdom

China has had the world's largest bureaucracy for over two thousand years. In imperial times, officials at every level owed their allegiance to the emperor; nowadays the focus of power is the communist leadership. The old saying had it that 'heaven is high, the emperor is far away', and for many Chinese, especially in the rural areas, the pattern of authority is still much the same as it was in imperial times. Power politics at the centre is invariably carried out behind closed doors, and decisions are announced to the populace in esoteric language. It is the local official who is the authority, rather than the Central Committee of the CP or a published constitution. Local officials are responsible for implementing the policies and initiatives that emanate from the capital, and the effectiveness of government depends considerably on them.

State and Party

The government of the Chinese state and the CP organization are, in theory at least, separate. Each has its own structure of representation and command, and each takes responsibility for different areas of Chinese life. The two organizations are much closer in practice. All the top state leaders are CP members, and are thus bound by Party loyalty and discipline. Whichever individual or faction is supreme within the Party also sets state policy. In the 1980s Deng Xiaoping, assisted first by younger lieutenants and then by an advisory council of his peers, had effective control of all government decisions.

People's Liberation Army

The third major force in Chinese public life, after the state and the Party, is the People's Liberation Army (PLA). The huge standing army is a potent force in domestic politics, and the civilian leadership is dependant on it to stay in power. China's elderly leaders seek to ensure the loyalty of the army by having relatives in key positions. The post of chairman of the Central Military Commission, effectively commander-in-chief of the army, is a vital one, and it is significant that this was the last position to be relinquished by Deng Xiaoping, well after he had placed younger colleagues at the head of the Party and state apparatus.

Before the massacres of June 1989, the army had not been turned on unarmed Chinese civilians (though it had been used against the Tibetans). Its actions severely damaged its prestige with the Chinese people, while making it indispensible to the leadership.

State organization

National People's Congress

The National People's Congress (NPC) is sometimes (rather misleadingly) described as China's parliament. Supposed to meet every five years, the NPC has representation from all regions and nationalities. Its mandate is to amend and enforce the constitution and to select the people who will hold the major offices of state. These include the largely ceremonial office of president, as well as the chairman of the Central Military Commission, the presidents of the Supreme Court and the Procuratorate, and the premier, who heads the state organization. In practice, the NPC merely approves constitutional changes and major appointments already decided by the leadership, and thus its role is principally symbolic.

State Council

The NPC has a Standing Committee, which meets periodically between congresses, but the principal work of government is performed by the State Council, the highest organ of state administration, headed by the premier. The post of state premier was held from 1949 until his death in 1976 by modern China's greatest statesman, Zhou Enlai.

Ministries

The State Council oversees the work of the state commissions (or super-ministries) and ministries that take responsibility for national policies. The commissions include defence, education, science, family planning, and economic restructuring. Ministries include finance, foreign affairs, foreign economic relations and trade, agriculture, communications and culture. Also controlled by the State

Council are organizations dealing with tourism, CAAC and the petrochemical and automotive industries, and the Special Economic Zone Office, which both oversees the SEZs (see Business) and acts as an advisory body on foreign investment in China.

CPPCC The China People's Political Consultative Conference (CPPCC) is a largely symbolic body which recognizes China's eight officially sanctioned democratic parties. The eight parties, no longer very active or democratic, are remnants from pre-1949 days, and their delegates are increasingly elderly. Attempts have been made in recent years to perpetuate these token democratic parties by recruiting younger members.

The democratic parties are joined in the CPPCC by national and religious minorities, overseas Chinese, and delegates representing Hong Kong and Taiwan. An indication of the limited influence of the CPPCC is that the role assigned to it is to 'help state organs carry out [Communist] Party policy'.

The parties represented in the CPPCC have nothing to do with the movement for democracy which sprang up in the 1980s in China's cities and among Chinese scholars studying in the West. The central authorities regard Western concepts of democracy with suspicion and hostility, and suppress them ruthlessly at home. Two major democratic parties among Chinese overseas are the Federation for a Democratic China (based in Paris) and the Chinese Alliance for Democracy (based in Washington).

Regional governments At the administrative level below the central government are the three municipalities of Beijing, Shanghai and Tianjin, twenty-two provinces (one more if Taiwan is included), and five 'autonomous regions' in the national minority areas. Each of these has its own structure of government, as do the prefectures, cities, districts and counties which bring government to the local level. Though it is the central administration in the capital that sets policy, the lower levels of government have considerable autonomy, and may either resist new policies or carry them farther and faster than the State Council plans. In matters of economic reform, for example, Guangdong (which surrounds Hong Kong) has pushed ahead of other provinces, frustrating the central authorities' attempts at overall planned development.

Communist Party

The Communist Party, which has governed China since 1949, is the most powerful organization in Chinese society, with some 48 million members. The CP was founded in 1921 at a secret meeting of twelve Chinese revolutionaries and some foreign advisers in Shanghai.

Congresses

That meeting was the first Party Congress, and the Party has held occasional congresses since then, the thirteenth taking place in 1987. Congresses have typically been held after a period of intense debate or factional fighting within the Party, and their purpose has been to consolidate the position of the dominant group by announcing changes in leadership or policy directions. The CP attempts to present a united front at all times, so factional struggles are fought, and compromises struck, behind the scenes in the months leading up to a congress.

Central Committee

The congresses ratify the composition of the Central Committee of the CP, which is convened for periodic plenary sessions. A smaller politburo meets more frequently; major decisions are most often made by an individual or very small group.

General secretary

The head of the CP was formerly given the title chairman, a post held by Mao Zedong for forty years until his death in 1976. He was succeeded by Hua Guofeng, who was briefly Party chairman, premier and chairman of the Central Military Commission, in an unprecedented but short-lived concentration of power. The title of chairman is no longer used, and the Party is headed instead by its general secretary. Hu Yaobang and Zhao Ziyang, who held the post of general secretary in the 1980s, were both seen as potential successors to Deng Xiaoping as China's most powerful leader, but were dismissed for their failure to handle dissent. The present general secretary is Jiang Zemin, the former mayor of Shanghai.

Cadres Like the state government, the CP has a chain of command from the centre to the local levels. The officials entrusted with carrying out CP initiatives are called cadres (*ganbu*) or Party cadres (*dang ganbu*). In rural China, the Party branch secretary controls his area with a combination of the pre-modern roles of the local gentry and the county magistrate. Peasants are still more likely to hope for an 'upright official' than to rely on the law to protect them. In the cities, the Party Committee of a factory, school, hospital or other institution is both a policy enforcer and a watchdog. Though recent central decisions have given more authority to managers and entrepreneurs throughout China, it is still the cadres who have the power to license and monitor enterprises, and to enforce new regulations (or not, as they choose). As a result, their power remains considerable.

The CP's ups and downs The Communist Party has had a turbulent history. Primarily an urban party in its early years, it allied itself with the ruling Nationalist Party in a united front against powerful regional warlords. Then in 1927, the CP was decimated in massacres ordered by Nationalist leader Chiang Kai-shek. While some members of the CP remained underground in the cities, others including Mao Zedong withdrew to rural bases in south-central China. They were driven from these bases in 1935 and forced to embark on the perilous Long March, a running battle fought over six thousand miles and ending in Yan'an, in the mountains of the north-west. After a second united front, this time against Japan in the Second World War, the Communists defeated the Nationalists and gained power over the country in 1949.

For the next thirty years, the group that had won the civil war was torn apart by a series of internecine struggles and purges. Some of those purged perished in the mid-1960s, in the violence of the Cultural Revolution. Others, like Deng Xiaoping, survived and returned to power in the late 1970s. The Cultural Revolution was halted by the death of Mao and the arrest of his widow Jiang Qing and her associates (called the 'Gang of Four') in 1976. Further purges

'Corruption' by Morgan Chua (The small figure facing the Great Wall is Deng Xiaoping.)

followed in the power-struggles of the 1980s, though top officials who find themselves demoted and denounced are rather more humanely treated by their colleagues than was the case under Mao.

By the late 1970s the CP's violent swings had exhausted much of the goodwill it had earned in the early years of the People's Republic as the provider of stability, sufficiency and self-respect to the Chinese people. Since the Party and its leadership had initiated mass campaigns like the Great Leap and the Cultural Revolution, they were inevitably tarnished by the havoc and misery these campaigns caused.

In 1979–80, articles and stories critical of the CP appeared in the Chinese press, none more trenchant than the writings of the investigative journalist and short-story writer Liu Binyan. As a young man in 1956, Liu had been expelled from the Party and sent into internal exile for portraying cadres as craven and self-seeking. He was reinstated twenty-three years later, and returned to prominence with an investigative report into a corruption case which set the tone for the literature of the early 1980s. In his report, *People or Monsters?*, Liu described how cadres formed relationships based on self-interest, bribed each other with embezzled state property, and protected each other from punishment when their corruption was exposed. 'The Communist Party regulated everything', Liu wrote, 'only it would not regulate the Communist Party.'

Liu's personal history is evidence of the CP's inability to tolerate its critics, and also of the different degrees of punishment it imposes at different times. In 1988 he was expelled from the Party again, this time for attacking its preference for blind obedience over more discerning loyalty. On this occasion, his 'banishment' was to Harvard as a visiting scholar. Liu has remained in the West, and has been one of the most outspoken and articulate critics of the June 1989 massacres and subsequent repression.

During the 1980s, the CP was regarded with ambivalence by many Chinese: applauded for its belated steps towards economic and social reform, but still mistrusted by many for the arbitrariness and corruption of many of its officials. In China, as in the Soviet Union, attempts by the top leadership to reform and restructure the Party were often thwarted by those who saw their own interests threatened, or who feared that any liberalization would set the Party on the road to its downfall.

The CP's violent crackdown on the democratic movement and the fall of communist regimes in Eastern Europe have combined to lead many of China's citizens to question the legitimacy of the CP's hold on power. The CP enters the 1990s still claiming to be a truly socialist party, but as one of the world's last totalitarian communist governments.

Coping with cadres

Foreigners who make their way into the wider Chinese society beyond the tour-bus and the hotel will quickly encounter cadre behaviour. Those doing business will run into factory committees, diplomats will lock horns with bureaucrats, and students and teachers will find their lives influenced by the Foreign Affairs Office of their institutions. Solo travellers will have to visit the PSB for travel documents.

Cadres, like officials everywhere, maintain their positions by not making waves. In cases where a show of initiative is likely to cause trouble, cadres will generally prefer to do nothing. Foreigners should be sensitive to this, respect the pressures that the cadres themselves are under, and avoid trying to force them to go out on a limb. When circumstances permit, cadres can be polite, well informed and obliging. Solo travellers often find that the PSB officials who handle travel permits will tell them more about a place than CITS.

Chinese officials pay attention to rank. A group of students accompanied by a professor is more likely to have activities arranged and problems solved by their Foreign Affairs Office than a group consisting only of students; similarly, a business delegation led by a company president is more likely to be respectfully received than one composed entirely of more junior personnel.

When trouble looms, as it does from time to time when foreigners live, work and study in China, the cadres in charge may act swiftly to solve problems. But you should not be surprised if they temporize in hopes that the matter will go away, refer it to an unavailable higher authority, vanish, or do the minimum possible to mollify the person with whom they are dealing.

Foreigners who are going to live in China need to learn how to work with cadres. The alternative is to waste time and energy in battles that cannot be won. Respect, charm and extreme persistence are the best ways of dealing with uncooperative cadres – if it is more trouble not to help than to help, the cadre may become obliging. If someone is being impossibly and unnecessarily obstructive, foreigners can often refer the matter to higher authorities (something few Chinese can do) in hopes that the difficulty they are facing can be overcome.

Trouble: making, avoiding and dealing with it

Many of the problems that foreigners encounter in China are of their own making, and can be avoided with care and foresight. Some will be familiar to anyone who has travelled at all extensively, while others are peculiar to China.

Health problems

Almost everyone who goes to China gets sick at some stage. The climate is not what they are used to, the food is unfamiliar, and they may come in contact with germs and viruses against which they have no immunity. Precautions can be taken to prevent minor ailments from inconveniencing you too much. More serious illnesses occur occasionally and should not be left untreated.

Minor ailments: prevention and treatment

North China is dry and dusty. The air in Beijing also carries the sand of the Gobi desert, automobile emissions and industrial pollutants. Many of its residents, and most of those who pass through, suffer from sore throats, hacking coughs and bronchitis. Go to Beijing well armed with throat lozenges, nasal decongestants and, if you are at all prone to sinus infections, a supply of whatever antibiotic you prefer. The residents of the capital often wear cloth face-masks when they go out in the winter. These are readily available, and screen out much of the dust and sand.

Winters in central and southern China can feel very cold because of the damp. In addition to warm and waterproof clothes and shoes, cold remedies are recommended. Summers can be very hot throughout China. Sunscreen and a hat are essential for those who come from temperate climates. An insect repellant is also useful.

Pollution and changes in climate from city to city combine to make respiratory ailments a common occurrence among travellers in China. Another cause of these problems is that the excitement of being in China makes people over-exert themselves, so that they stay up later, get busy earlier and walk longer distances than they do at home. Over-exertion is dangerous, especially for older travellers who customarily lead quiet lives; the risk is that by trying to do without sufficient rest in the first few days of a tour they can ruin their own trips and inconvenience their fellow travellers.

Rich food, spicy food, unhygienic food or merely unfamiliar food can cause diarrhoea. China's public facilities, especially in out-of-the-way places, are not for queasy stomachs. If you do not travel with diarrhoea remedies, you can experiment with Chinese traditional medicines. However, a day or two of rice and boiled water is probably as effective as any medication.

Constipation is a frequent complaint when people suddenly start to eat rice two or even three times a day. Fruit is a useful antidote (peel it first!), and there are remedies you can take to China with you. Otherwise, you might try a visit to a Chinese pharmacy. The constipation treatments are swiftly effective.

Major ailments

Persistent and serious health problems should be treated by a doctor. Many hotels, colleges and universities have clinics with doctors trained in Western medicine. Even those who cannot communicate in English should know English names for most diseases and will prescribe Western medicines. Hospitals will offer Western patients the best facilities they have, though conditions and treatment may seem primitive by the standards of more affluent nations. Costs for attention and medicine are generally low, but you will be required to pay on the spot. If you are concerned about the quality of sterilization, take your own syringes. You should be aware that there is a slight risk of infection from acupuncture needles, which are seldom adequately sterilized.

Major cities have hospitals designated to receive foreign patients. In Beijing, go to the Capital Hospital just off Wangfujing Street; in Shanghai, to the Number 1 Hospital on North Suzhou Road; in Guangzhou, to the Number 1 Hospital on North Renmin Road. These are among the best hospitals in China. Foreign patients are a valuable source of foreign exchange for these hospitals, and charges can be as high as private health-care in the West. There have been cases where foreign patients have been asked to pay fairly large sums in FECs and even US dollars before a doctor will see them. Such practices are not standard (though Chinese patients often do have to pay in advance), but it is as well to be prepared. You will be asked to pay before you leave, and should be certain to get receipts so that you can recover expenditures from your insurance company.

Medical problems requiring long-term hospitalization and all but emergency surgery are best dealt with at home. Chinese doctors tend to over-treat foreign patients to reassure them that everything possible is being done. Post-operative therapy is almost nonexistent.

Emergency In the case of serious illness or the death of a companion, call the embassy or consulate of your country. Helping in such cases is one of the reasons they are there.

Innoculations Innoculations are not mandatory for travel to China. However, there are diseases that are endemic in China for which preventive measures can be considered. Meningitis, encephalitis, hepatitis and malaria are the more serious of these diseases, and you should see a doctor immediately if you suspect you have symptoms.

Dental care Methods of dentistry are not as advanced as most Westerners are used to. The best treatment can be found at the dental schools attached to major teaching hospitals. People who will be in China for any length of time should see their own dentist and have necessary work done before they go.

Police problems and problem behaviour

Foreigners in China, especially foreign residents, are closely monitored, and should not consider breaking the law any more than they would in their own country. Changing money illegally, dealing in black-market goods and taking photographs where forbidden (airports, military installations) should be avoided.

Foreign residents who read and speak Chinese should be careful about handling documents that are *neibu*, 'internal', and receiving or passing on information that might be classified. Much 'internal' information is generally known through the grapevine, and Chinese people are less likely than foreigners to know what information is going to be officially regarded as sensitive. It is important to consider the effect on Chinese friends if illegal behaviour is discovered or suspected – the punishment is invariably much harsher for a Chinese person than for a foreigner.

Cases of theft, assault, and accident involving injury should be reported to the PSB, who will deal with them as fully as they can. More common police trouble results from visa and traffic infractions. Here the correct attitude is one of humble amiability. About the worst that can happen to people that are where they should not be is that they will be required to write a confession of their misdeeds and put on a bus back to where they came from. In the case of a cycling or traffic offence, the policeman may enjoy chastising a foreigner so much that he'll leave it at that.

In addition to not taking illegal pictures, photographers should exercise the same discretion and good manners they would at home. In particular, ask permission before photographing soldiers, the elderly and members of minority nationalities (any of whom may well say no). Irate tribesmen have threatened violence when provoked by rude photographers!

Mechanical problems

If you are going to be spending a long time in China, try not to take anything that is both indispensable and unfixable. Most mechanical things (radios, bicycles, non-electronic watches) can be mended as well, and much more cheaply, in China than outside. More sophisticated electronic equipment presents greater problems because of unfamiliarity to Chinese repairmen and unavailability of spare parts. Personal computers should be sent to Hong Kong for repair, though the IBM office in Beijing will repair IBM systems. Some young entrepreneurs have set up computer-repair companies, some of which offer good service; they are unlicensed by the makers, however, and so you use them at your own risk. Of foreign cars, Toyotas are probably the most familiar to repairmen. Household appliances can be mended as well (or as badly) in China as outside.

Repairmen are in great demand, and Chinese families who call one may well be expected to feed him, offer a gift and even arrange transportation on top of the going rate for the service. A foreigner who might be needing further repairs should consider some similar demonstration of appreciation.

Delays Chinese people have a high tolerance for delays and long waits, which is the result of long practice. Getting angry if a plane is delayed or a ticket cannot be booked usually achieves very little. Polite persistence will sometimes enable you to find the cause of the delay, if not speed things up. In case all else fails, be prepared with a long book.

Getting lost Non-Chinese speakers venturing into the unknown should take with them a label or envelope with the name of their hotel, which they can show to people on the street in case they need to get directions back. Buy a street map of a city; then if you lose your way or want to know where you are, stand on a street corner, open the map, look puzzled and wait for the crowd to form around you. Quite probably someone will speak English; equally probably there will be half a dozen suggestions as to your best route. Frequently someone will guide you. It's a situation which brings out the charm and hospitality of the Chinese man and woman on the street.

Business

Since the beginning of the Deng era in 1978, China's economy has been dominated by a series of wide-ranging reforms. The old system of central planning, learned from the Soviet Union in the 1950s, emphasized state-controlled heavy industry and the collectivization of agriculture. It was replaced to a considerable extent by a system allowing greater autonomy to the regions and encouraging greater initiative to individuals and businesses. Foreign business was welcomed for its capital and technology, both of which China needed to achieve modernization of the economy.

After the reforms were introduced, the Chinese economy grew at an unprecedented rate, almost ten per cent per annum during the 1980s. The reforms were also successful in raising personal incomes and stimulating consumer demand. However, these achievements were not without cost: the growth of the economy also led to a balance of payment deficit and inflation of twenty per cent per annum in the second part of the decade. In 1988 the government moved to reduce imports and restrict the money supply as a means of bringing the economy under control.

Many of the advocates of economic reform also favoured a measure of political relaxation. Chief among them was Zhao Ziyang, who served first as state premier and then as CP general secretary in the 1980s. When Zhao was removed from office in June 1989 for his conciliatory approach to the democracy movement, many of his reform-minded associates and advisers were also dismissed or demoted. They have been replaced by more conservative and centralist economic planners. However, the economic reforms of the 1980s had gone too far to be rolled back entirely, and the leadership continues to recognize the need for both home-grown entrepreneurs and foreign businesspeople.

Responsibility and entrepreneurship

Domestically, economic reform has been spearheaded by the 'responsibility system'. In the countryside, this has meant the disbanding of the agricultural communes set up in the late 1950s, and allowing peasant families to contract with the state to farm land or operate rural industries. The contract-holder is responsible for providing the state with a quota of produce or goods, and can dispose of any surplus on the open market. Small-scale industries in the villages and country towns of rural China have increased local incomes and employed millions of peasants whose labour is not needed on the farm.

Entrepreneurs in rural and urban China have been encouraged to set up businesses, principally in the service sector. High achievers, or 'ten thousand *yuan* households', have been praised in the Chinese press, though their successes have infected many of their neighbours and local officials with the 'red-eye disease' of jealousy.

In industry and commerce, the 'managerial responsibility system' has allowed individual managers greater power, and less interference from Party committees, as long as they turn a profit. Some managers have leased state-owned enterprises such as department stores, and shared increased profits with their workforce. Businesses that fail have been allowed to go bankrupt rather than being baled out by the state.

The economic and political retrenchment of the late 1980s and early 90s, particularly the limits set on credit and imports, have hurt many of China's new entrepreneurs. Many of them were also vocal supporters of the democracy movement of spring 1989, and have come under increasing scrutiny since the movement's suppression. There have been accusations of tax evasion and exploitation of workers, and many private businesses have been closed down.

Consumer demand

Higher earnings have increased consumer expectations, and some foreign products are in particularly high demand. In the early 1980s most brides expected their husband's family to provide a watch, sewing-machine, bicycle and radio, all of which could be Chinese brands. Now the request is more likely to be for a refrigerator, washing-machine, colour TV and cassette recorder, preferably all made overseas. To date, Japanese manufacturers have led the way in supplying these articles, due to their aggressive pursuit of Chinese markets through extensive and effective advertising.

Upwardly mobile urban Chinese are also developing tastes for Western delights like sliced bread and fast food. Coke and Pepsi, luxury items at around 2 *yuan* a can and 5 *yuan* for a two-litre bottle, are high-status drinks. These new consumer trends are a product of the infiltration of the Chinese market by Western companies which the economic policies of the reformers encouraged.

Western business and China

Western attitudes towards China as a place to do business typically swing from extreme optimism to acute frustration. The optimism was clearest during US president Ronald Reagan's visit to (in his words) 'this so-called communist country' in 1984, when he predicted that hundreds of thousands of Americans would soon be working in China, and presumably making healthy profits in a booming economy. In practice, the Chinese were not seeking to internationalize their economy in the way Reagan envisaged. While they needed (and continue to need) what Western business had to offer, they had no intention of losing control to foreign capital, as has happened in other developing countries. Frustration with doing

Mr Yang says China is vast, the China Market is vast, your opportunities are vast — so it should not be such a surprise that our bureaucracy is also vast

This cartoon first appeared in the November/December issue of *The China Business Review*, and has been reprinted with permission of the US–China Business Council

business in China is most often seen in complaints about the byzantine Chinese bureaucracy, constant political interference, arbitrary price increases, and the enormous time it takes to get anything done.

China business: pros and cons

The attractions of China for foreign business are obvious:

With a population of well over a thousand million and an expanding economy, China represents a huge and largely unexploited market for foreign goods.

The Chinese leadership's enthusiasm for the biggest and most modern in technology and industrial development raises the prospect of state mega-projects which will need enormous foreign participation. The largest of these, the massive Three Gorges hydro-electric dam on the Yangtze River, is now on hold, but China's economic planners recently announced a project that will see ten power stations constructed on the Wujiang (a tributary of the Yangtze) to supply power to the south-west.

With its large surplus workforce, relatively low wages and incentives to foreign business, China has great potential as the site for factories producing goods for Asian and world markets.

With a growing contingent of overseas Chinese and foreign businesspeople and tourists expecting international standards of accommodation and service, there are opportunities for those wishing to meet their needs.

It was in this final respect that the overseas investors of the early 1980s were most successful, though later projects have suffered from a saturated market and reduced demand. Some manufacturing branch-plants, particularly those producing merchandise for international markets, have fared well, but others have been money-losers. In 1986, a review of foreign investment concluded that: 'the allure of China as a country in which to invest is still not substantiated by the facts', and subsequent events have generally borne out that conclusion. Some recurrent problems associated with doing business in China are:

While the potential market really is huge, the disposable income of most Chinese remains low; their purchasing power is in RMB, which cannot be taken out of the country.

A tradition of guaranteed employment (the so-called 'iron rice-bowl') and low wages have resulted in a workforce with limited skills and motivation. In addition to the hidden costs of extensive benefit packages prescribed by the state, many foreign employers have found it necessary to pay bonuses to their staff simply for showing up to work.

The Chinese economy, industry in particular, has developed more rapidly than the infrastructure can support. Transportation, communications and power generation, especially away from the main centres, are inadequate.

The Chinese legal system frequently deals with disputes between Chinese and foreign enterprises by imposing solutions which are patriotic or politically expedient, rather than in accordance with the conventions of international law.

China has many levels of government, all of which want a share of whatever can be squeezed out of the overseas investor. Foreign businesses are regularly hit with arbitrary and unexpected price increases for office rentals, power, salaries, etc., as local governments and enterprises strive to maximize profits. Since Chinese units have little influence over each other, and the central government generally chooses not to intervene, the foreign business has the choice of paying up or pulling out, a situation which places a strain on the resources and the goodwill of many foreign companies.

Special Economic Zones

Since 1980, foreign companies have been able to locate and do business in Special Economic Zones (SEZs). The first SEZ was established in 1979 at Shenzhen, near the border with Hong Kong. Three more opened for business the following year, at Xiamen (Amoy), Shantou (Swatow) and Zhuhai, also on the south coast.

The SEZs were the testing-ground for China's economic reforms. They are characterized by freer movement of money to and from the outside world, substantial tax-concessions for foreign industries in their start-up phase, and a better trained and better paid workforce. They were set up to attract foreign technology and investment, and to challenge the economic might of the region's 'four dragons' (Hong Kong, South Korea, Taiwan and Singapore). A visiting Deng Xiaoping is said to have remarked on a visit to Shenzhen in 1984 that 'time is money, productivity is life', an indication of how far the new leadership had come from the revolutionary rhetoric of Mao Zedong. The speed of expansion of the SEZs was curbed the following year after massive corruption came to light, but development has continued, especially of high-tech industries.

In 1984, districts in fourteen coastal cities (including Shanghai, Tianjin and Guangzhou) were opened to SEZ-style business practices. Most recently, redevelopment has begun in Shanghai's Pudong district, where massive foreign participation is being sought for a new commercial and light-industrial zone.

Joint Ventures

Many of the most conspicuous and capital-intensive economic projects of the 1980s have been the work of Joint Ventures (JVs). JVs are companies created by a contractual agreement between Chinese and foreign interests. Typically, the foreign side supplies technology, plant and capital, and the Chinese side land (which is leased rather than sold to the JV) and labour. The company is jointly run, the Chinese staff being trained by the foreign partner. The contracts for JVs to date have averaged fourteen years, after which the foreign partner withdraws, leaving the company and the profits to the Chinese side.

Since the Chinese partner is a company and not the state, a newly-formed JV still has to apply for a licence to export its products, and must pay substantial levies on materials imported into China, and heavy commercial taxes (unless it is located in a SEZ and can take advantage of the tax-concessions there).

The government's purpose in allowing JVs to set up was principally to finance long-term projects with high capital costs, for example in mining and other resource industries. To date, the majority of JVs have been in construction and manufacturing, which hold the promise of a speedier return on investment.

Among the most successful of the early JVs was the Jianguo Hotel in Beijing, the first hotel to be built as a JV (the partners in this case being Chinese-Americans and CITS), which recouped its original investment of US$22 million in only three years. The Jianguo has been promoted throughout China as a model of hotel management.

Other JVs have had their problems. Also in Beijing, the Noble Tower office complex, begun at the same time as the Jianguo, was an object lesson in what can go wrong with a JV if the two sides (the Chinese-Canadian Noble Chong Asia Ltd. and the China International Science Centre) mistrust each other. There were disputes over the payment of unanticipated increased charges for power, tenants' security deposits and parking facilities, over the design of the buildings and even the name of the complex. These disputes resulted in delays, strained relations between the partners and economic losses before the complex was completed.

The most publicized and best documented of all the JVs has been the American Motors Company's JV to manufacture jeeps in China. The ups and downs of Beijing Jeep are documented in a book-length study (listed in Further Reading).

Changes to the rules for setting up JVs, designed to encourage more foreign businesses to sign JV contracts, have recently been proposed. Should these changes come into effect, the limits on the life of a JV will be removed, giving the foreign side longer to recoup its investment and make a profit.

Getting in and setting up

Over the past decade, a number of overseas companies have set up offices in China. To date, the majority have been in Beijing, since location in the capital gives access to Chinese government departments, such as the Ministry of Foreign Relations and Trade, and the Bank of China. It also means that the foreign businesses are nearer their nations' embassies. Beijing is one of the world's most expensive cities in which to do business. Office rentals are at least twice as high as those in Hong Kong, and may be raised without notice.

Other foreign companies operate in Shanghai (China's largest port and still just about the major industrial city), Guangzhou (China's link with Hong Kong and South-East Asia) and, increasingly, the SEZs. Office space is tight here as well, though less so than in Beijing.

Three useful acronyms

MOFERT The Ministry of Foreign Economic Relations and Trade, is the Chinese government agency which handles dealings with foreign business. It was set up in 1982 by amalgamating four existing foreign trade organizations.

CITIC China International Trust and Investment Company, was set up in 1979 under businessmen prominent in the 1940s but dispossessed, condemned and in many cases jailed for much of the first thirty years of the People's Republic. CITIC's mandate is to manage investment and financing for projects in China.

FESCO The Foreign Enterprise Staff Corporation, is a government agency (actually an office of the Public Security Bureau) which hires out employees to foreign companies, keeps over 70 per cent of their salaries and requires them to report on their employers' activities. It is not popular with most foreign businesspeople.

Making contact

If you intend to do business with China but have no contacts, a useful first step is to enquire at the departments of your own government which handle trade relations. They may have up-to-date information on trends and regulations for China business, and equally usefully, they may know of Chinese delegations in your field which may be travelling outside China and hoping to establish relations with foreign businesses.

Personal contact is a very important part of establishing a business relationship in China. Alternative sources of this kind of information are organizations like the Sino-British Trade Council, The National Council for US–China Trade and the Canada–China Trade Council (see Useful Addresses). Chinese embassies and consulates also have commercial attaches whose responsibilities include introducing Chinese and foreign businesses to each other.

Delegations and presentations

A company wishing to visit potential partners or customers in China, to mount an exhibition of products or conduct technical seminars, must first be invited by a Chinese 'host' organization, which will make most of the arrangements.

Delegations should be led by an executive of the highest possible rank, and include one member with a good command of Mandarin, or Cantonese if the target region is Guangzhou or Guangdong province. Business cards printed in Chinese on one side and English on the other are an asset and a mark of courtesy to Chinese hosts. The printing job can be done by printers in Western Chinatowns or in Hong Kong. A rule of thumb is to take three times as many business cards as you think you will need.

The business seminar has been compared to a blind date, and the foreign businessperson generally has little idea who will attend a seminar. For the Chinese side, such occasions offer the opportunity to learn about the most up-to-date foreign technology at the exhibitor's expense. Exhibitors can expect to be grilled at considerable length on their merchandise, and should go to China with more brochures and promotional materials than they think they could possibly use. Some of the materials should be translated into Chinese, and a better than adequate technical interpreter is extremely valuable.

Banquets

Banquets are an established part of setting up and maintaining business relationships. On a promotional tour, at least one banquet should be hosted by the foreign company. The 'host' organization or a hotel management can recommend a restaurant and make reservations. The visitor, as host of the banquet, will be given a choice of *biaozhun* (standard price).

A higher *biaozhun* may not noticeably improve the quality of the meal, but the guests will know how much was paid and appreciate an expensive meal as a tribute to their importance.

At the banquet, the highest-ranking executive of the foreign company, as host, takes the seat at head table which faces the door, with his/her Chinese counterpart to the right, and the next in command to the left, with interpreters in between if necessary. Chinese officials are very conscious of rank, and attention should be paid to this kind of protocol. Place-cards printed with a company logo and inscribed for the event ensure that everyone is properly seated. Toasts can be proposed at regular intervals and will be responded to, but the Chinese injunction to *ganbei* 'dry the glass' need not be taken too seriously. Drunkenness is frowned on, and Chinese rice-spirits are extremely potent, especially if mixed with other drinks. The Chinese business elite is becoming increasingly cosmopolitan, and the range of subjects open for dinner-table discussion is broad; jokes about sex, however, are best avoided.

Conducting negotiations

A cordial personal relationship based on mutual respect is a prerequisite for business dealings. Chinese negotiators are prepared for hard bargaining, but react with hostility to what they perceive as impatience, arrogance or bullying. Their aim is to secure the best possible deal for themselves, in a way that will leave both parties content and neither resentful. Over the ten years of increased foreign contacts, the Chinese have developed a cadre of tough and sophisticated business negotiators. Western executives should be prepared to encounter any or all of the following negotiating techniques from their Chinese counterparts, all of which have been used to good effect in dealing with foreign companies:

demanding a favorable deal because China is a poor country compared to the rich Western nation the foreign business represents.

appeals to friendship, personal, institutional or national, or, in the case of overseas Chinese, 'patriotism'.

indirect references to the historical exploitation of China by foreign nations. This guilt-inducing tactic was initially successful with the Japanese, who occupied much of North China during the Second World War. Younger Japanese businessmen are less disposed to feel the burden of history.

the promise of massive future profit if the foreign investor is willing to lose in the short term. Come-ons like 'if only one Chinese in ten buys a car . . .' are fantasies and no business decisions should be based on them.

endless stalling over details after the main points of a deal have been agreed and the Western partner is in a hurry to get home.

insistence, after deals are signed, that all unanticipated costs be paid by the foreign company, since the bills are in foreign currency, which the Chinese side does not hold.

Establishing a presence

If there are genuine prospects of long-term benefit, opening a China office, despite the expense, is the next step. Foreign businesses operating in China need to be registered with the Administration of Industry and Commerce (AIC). Application for this must be made through a Chinese 'host' organization. The foreign company's representative must be named in the application, and a registration fee will be charged. The 'host' organization is held responsible by the Chinese authorities for the conduct of the foreign 'guest'.

Keeping up to date

China business information becomes outdated quickly. While the books mentioned in Further reading give valuable background information, the following journals are also recommended: For China business in the context both of socio-political change and Asia business, *The Far Eastern Economic Review* and *The Asian Wall Street Journal* are indispensible. *The China Business Review* (published by the US–China Business Council in Washington), and *The Sino-British Trade Review* (from the Sino-British Trade Council in London) are specialist journals dealing with bilateral trade. The Chinese magazine *China Market* (published in Hong Kong) combines advertisements with short articles and business news items.

Language

English An epidemic of what the Chinese call 'English fever' began in the early 1980s and is still raging. Mastery of the English language is seen as desirable for personal advancement, and for gaining access to the previously forbidden fruits of Western culture. For a fortunate few, the language is essential for study abroad.

English is taught at most primary and secondary schools as well as in colleges and universities. Employees of hotels, restaurants and businesses serving foreigners also learn appropriate English conversation. Outside the formal educational system, there is instruction in English on the radio, much of it geared to getting through the TOEFL test. English-speaking clubs for part-time learners have activities and competitions; the winner of the 1988 English Recital Contest in Beijing performed a 'vivid imitation of a banquet speech by British Prime Minister Margaret Thatcher'.

The result of this 'English fever' is that the visitor who stays in major centres can generally function comfortably in English. Interpreters are available for businesspeople, tour-guides usually speak English well, and in case of need there is often someone with enough of the language to help out. These days there are millions of Chinese people who are keen to practise such English as they know on a Western visitor. We believe, however, that it is still advisable for visitors, particularly those who venture outside the areas most frequented by foreigners, to equip themselves with the bare essentials of survival Chinese.

Chinese Learning Chinese can be an intimidating prospect. Unlike Western languages, Chinese is tonal, which means that the tone, or inflection, of a sound can alter the meaning that sound represents. In addition, the spoken language is not the same in different parts of the country. A Shanghainese man speaking his own dialect cannot make himself understood in Guangzhou, while someone from Guangzhou would meet with incomprehension and even ridicule in Beijing. In some parts of rural China, even the dialects of neighbouring counties may not be mutually comprehensible. To complicate matters further, the written language bears no resemblance to a Western script, since it is composed of characters, which represent both sound and meaning, rather than words made up of letters which together indicate a sound.

Achieving mastery of Chinese is difficult – ask anyone who has taken a Chinese course – though it is probably no harder than learning English as a second language. However, learning to understand a few key phrases when they are spoken to you, picking up some survival Chinese and even recognizing some Chinese characters, are all quite possible with a little perseverance. Once you have a smattering of Chinese, the best way to learn more is to listen and practise what you know.

Mandarin

The language that foreigners should learn is standard Chinese, known in the West as Mandarin. Mandarin, which is called 'common speech' in China and 'the national language' in Taiwan, is based on the Beijing dialect, and is spoken throughout most of north China. It is the language taught at many Western universities and colleges. (It is not the language of most Western Chinatowns, however. These are dominated by the sounds of Cantonese, the dialect of the cities of Hong Kong and Guangzhou and the areas that surround them.)

Since the establishment of the People's Republic, all schoolchildren have been taught Mandarin. Films made in China are in Mandarin, as are the television programmes and radio programmes produced by the Central Broadcasting Station in Beijing. Virtually everyone in China can understand Mandarin, and all but the elderly can speak it, though this is not to say they all speak it well. Residents of south China must effectively be bilingual, speaking both their local dialect and the 'common speech'. Their Mandarin often has a strong regional accent, and may contain vocabulary and expressions common in their own dialect that do not exist in the standard speech.

Regional variations

The residents of Beijing tend to be very superior about their pronunciation of the spoken language, and delight in mocking other people's rendition of it. Impersonation of non-standard accents are a stock-in-trade of the comedians who perform *xiangsheng*, or comic dialogues, a popular entertainment in Beijing. For example, the Shanghainese word for 'wash' sounds like the Mandarin word for 'hit', which offers hilarious possibilities for a barber-shop joke in which the customer is from Beijing and the barber from Shanghai:

> I sat down in the chair and he said: 'Want a hit?' 'Do you always do that?' I asked. 'Hit 'em all!' he replied. I didn't want to go against the local customs, so I said, 'Okay then, you'd better hit me too' (slightly adapted from *Opera and Dialect*, by Hou Baolin, the king of the comic dialogue)

The people of the south-western province of Sichuan are also mocked for their failure to distinguish between an 'n' and an 'l' at the start of a word. Northerners find it comical that when a Sichuanese man wants to say that one of his children is male (*nan*) and one female (*nü*), he may end up claiming that his children are blue (*lan*) and green (*lü*).

Written language

The written language has been a unifying force through China's long history, since it can be read and understood by people who speak different dialects. Before the twentieth century, the small minority of educated people read and wrote a classical language which bore little relation to any spoken form. The May Fourth reformers of the early years of this century led the way in developing a written language based on standard speech, and their efforts resulted in the language that may be read today in newspapers, magazines and books.

Becoming literate in Chinese is an arduous business for a Chinese child, a fact that might be a small comfort to the non-Chinese student of Mandarin sweating over a dictionary or textbook. To be able to read a newspaper, magazine article or story without too much trouble, it is necessary to recognize about fifteen hundred of the characters that are the building-blocks of the written language. These characters, each of which corresponds to a syllable in the spoken language, combine to form words. Fifteen hundred characters can expand to a vocabulary of several thousand words.

Characters

The Chinese written tradition goes back over three thousand years. The earliest examples of characters still in existence are to be found etched on 'oracle bones', shoulder-blade bones of cattle used for making divinations in the second millennium BC. The script was standardized by the unifying Qin dynasty in the third century BC, and these full, or complex, characters remain in use today in Taiwan and Hong Kong.

Pictographs

The first Chinese characters were stylized versions of pictures of animals and other natural phenomena important to an emerging culture. These are called 'pictographs'. The picture ⊙ , now written 日 , represented the sun, and ☽ , now written 月 , the moon. [illegible] , now 人 , stood for man, and [illegible] , now 牛 , for cow.

Ideographs

To these 'pictographs' were added 'ideographs', characters which give an idea. The best examples of these are 一 , 二 , 三 , 'one, two, three', respectively.

Combined meanings

Further characters were creating by putting two images together within one character: the sun and the moon combine to give 明 , 'brightness'. The character 好 , which has a woman, 女 , on the left and a child, 子 , on the right means 'good' or 'to love'. A woman under the roof, 安 means 'peace', and a pig under the roof, 家 , is 'home'.

'Peace' and 'home' by Tan Huay Peng

Meaning and sound

The visual methods of creating characters described above have their limitations, and while the examples given are some of the commonest words in the language, the vast majority of characters are formed in another way – the combination of one part of a character which gives an idea of meaning (called a 'radical') with another which provides a clue to the sound (a 'phonetic'). Common radicals include 氵, 'water', seen for example in 河, 'river', and 洗, 'to wash', and 扌,'hand', as in 提, 'to lift', and 推, 'to push'.

The Chinese word for 'to weave' is 纺, pronounced *fang* in Mandarin. Its phonetic element (on the right) is *fang*, 方 , which on its own means 'square'. The radical of 'to weave' (on the left) is 纟 , 'silk'. So from looking at the character, it should be possible to guess that the word it represents is something to do with silk and sounds something like *fang*. Phonetics do not always give a very good idea of how a character should be pronounced. This is because the spoken language has changed a lot more than the written over the two or three thousand years that the characters have been in use.

Simplification

Chinese characters can be extremely complex; it takes sixteen strokes of the pen, brush or pencil to write 龍 , 'dragon', and eighteen to write 豐 , 'abundant'. These are two of the characters that have been simplified since the 1950s; they now read 龙 and 丰 respectively. The purpose of simplifying the written language is to make it easier for as many people as possible to learn to read, in contrast to the traditional society, where the written language was the preserve of the elite.

The new versions are certainly easier to learn, and officials responsible for teaching people the simplified characters reported that former illiterates jumped for joy when they found how easy writing could be. The simplifications are not without some drawbacks: sometimes a visual image is lost, as is the case when the character 東 , 'the east', a picture of the sun, 日 , coming up behind a tree, 木 , is simplified to 东 . Critics (both in China and outside) complain that by simplifying ancient characters, the language reformers are cutting the Chinese people off from their heritage. The Chinese government originally planned to keep on introducing new simplifications until all characters were written with ten strokes or less. However, no new simplified characters have been introduced for over ten years, and the process of simplification appears to have been halted.

Pinyin

A further goal of the language reformers of the 1950s was the 'Latinization' of the written language, meaning that eventually Chinese words would be written in letters rather than in characters. This aim seems to have been abandoned or at least shelved. Chinese sounds are frequently written in Western letters, however, in the pinyin or 'matched sounds' system used to teach Mandarin to speakers of non-standard dialects and to foreigners. Pinyin can be seen all over China, on shop-signs and product labels most of all, but generally in conjunction with characters. Children learn pinyin in elementary school, though most forget it soon after.

Chinese names in this book (except those that reflect non-Mandarin pronunciation) are given in pinyin. The older Wade-Giles romanization, seen in Western books and newspapers until the early 1980s, is now seldom used.

A Chinese word with a built-in story

Chinese words are generally made up of two characters whose own meanings combine to indicate the word. Some modern words have their origins in classical writings dating back hundreds of years. The Chinese word for 'contradiction' (a common word in a Marxist state) is *maodun*, which literally means 'spear (and) shield'. Its origin is in this story by the third-century BC philosopher Han Fei which appears in cartoon form on the next two pages.

There was a man selling weapons in the market. He held up a shield and said: 'My shields are so solid that no spear can pierce them.'

Then he picked up a spear and boasted. 'My spears are so sharp that no shield can withstand them.'

One of the onlookers asked: 'So what will happen if I use one of your spears against one of your shields?'

Tongue-tied and defeated, the seller gathered up his weapons and went home. Later on the expression 'using one's sword and shield against each other' came to mean contradicting oneself.

Survival Chinese

A few phrases of survival Chinese can be a life-saver. Your efforts to communicate in Chinese, however halting, will also be appreciated by the people you meet. There's no need to feel self-conscious – remember that to a speaker of standard Beijing Mandarin, a foreigner's mispronunciations are not going to sound any funnier than those of a southerner!

Pronunciation

Chinese words in this book are given in the pinyin system. Most of the letters are pronounced more or less as they are in English, with the exceptions listed below

Consonants

c as ts in 'bits'
q as ch in 'chin'
r somewhere between an 'r' and a 'j', said with the tongue on the roof of the mouth
x between English 's' and 'sh'

Vowels

ai as uy in 'guy'
ao as ow in 'now'
e as in 'her'
ei as ay in 'hay'
i as e in unstressed 'the' after c, ch, r, s, sh, z, zh; elsewhere as ee in 'see'
ian as 'yen'
o as in 'for'
ou as in 'dough'
u as o in 'do'
uo as au in English 'daughter'
ü, and u after j, q, x, as in the French word 'tu', spoken through pursed lips

Tones The marks that appear over words indicate the intonation with which they should be spoken. As a rough guide:

first tone – : a high level sound, like someone imitating the "toot" of a steam-train.
second tone ⁄ : a rising intonation, like a question.
third tone v: a sound that dips down, then slightly up again, as in disbelief.
fourth tone ∖ : a falling sound, with finality.

When a sound does not have one of these marks above it, it is 'unstressed' and pronounced lightly.

Tones make a big difference to meaning. The same sound with different tones can mean very different things. For example: *mā* (first tone) means 'mother'; *má* (second tone) means 'hemp' or 'marijuana'; *mǎ* (third tone) means 'horse'; *mà* (fourth tone) means 'to curse' or 'to scold'; and *ma* (unstressed) is put on the end of a statement to make it into a question.

Where possible, we have given expressions in a question-and-answer format, so you will have some idea of the conversations that are possible with limited Chinese. With appropriate gestures, these few expressions should get you started. The best way to learn a language is by hearing it spoken and trying it yourself. There are a thousand million people waiting to help!

Hail and farewell	Q: *ní hǎo?*	How are you?
	A: *hén hǎo, nǐ ne?*	Fine, and yourself?
	Q: *chī fàn le ma?*	Have (you) eaten?
	A: *chī fàn le*	(Yes, I) have eaten
	zàijiàn	Goodbye
Identity	Q: *guìxìng?*	What's your (honourable) surname?
	A: *wǒ xìng . . .*	My surname is . . .
	Q: *nǐ (shi) nǎguó rén?*	What country are you from?

A: *Wŏ shi . . .*	I'm . . .
Yīngguó rén	British
Aòdàlìyà rén	Australian
Jiānádà rén	Canadian
Mĕiguó rén	American

Note: Chinese people tell where they are from by saying the place-name plus *rén*, 'person'. So:

Wŏ shi . . .	I'm . . .
Bĕijīng rén	from Beijing
Shànghăi rén	Shanghainese
Guăngdōng rén	Cantonese

Introductions

wŏ jièshao yí xià	Let me make the introductions
zhèiwèi shi . . . zhèiwèi shi	This is . . . and this is . . .
jiúyăng	Delighted to meet you

Politeness

xièxie	Thank you

The correct response to '*xièxie*' is:

bié kèqi	Don't be so polite

duìbuqĭ	I'm sorry/excuse me

The correct response to '*duìbuqĭ*' is:

méi guānxi	It doesn't matter

Information

Q: *zhè shi shénme?*	What's this?
A: *nà shi . . .*	That's . . .
Q: *tā shi shéi?*	Who's he/she?
A: *tā shi . . .*	He/she's . . .
Q: *nĭ qù năr?*	Where are you going?
A: *wŏ qù . . .*	I'm going to . . .
Q: *zhèr yŏu méi yŏu . . . ?*	Is there a . . . here?
lüguăn	Guesthouse/hotel
fànguăn	Restaurant
cèsuŏ	Toilet
yīsheng	Doctor
yīyuàn	Hospital
rén huì Yīngwén	Someone who speaks English

Health	*wǒ bìng le*	I'm sick
	wǒ bù shūfu	I don't feel well
	wǒ . . . téng	My . . . hurts
	tóu	Head
	wèi	Stomach
	tuǐ	Leg
	wǒ dàbiàn bùtōng	I'm constipated
	wǒ lā dùzi	I have diarrhoea

Getting around	Q: *. . . zài nǎr?*	Where's the . . .?
	. . . zěnme zǒu?	How do you get to . . .?
	yǒuyì shāngdiàn	Friendship Store
	zìyóu shìchǎng	Free market
	huǒchēzhàn	Rail-station
	shòupiàochù	Ticket office
	yínháng	Bank
	Běijīng fàndiàn	Beijing Hotel
	A: *zài . . . biān*	(It's) to the . . .
	wàng . . . zǒu	(You) head to the . . .
	qián	Front
	hòu	Back
	dōng	East
	xī	West
	nán	South
	běi	North

On the phone	*wei*! (any tone, shout!)	Hello?
	qǐng jiē wàixiàn	Please give me an outside line
	qǐng jiē . . . fēnjī	Extension . . . please
	qǐng jiē sān-wǔ-èr fēnjī	Extention 352 please
	Q: *. . . zài ma?*	Is . . . there?
	A: *ní děng yì děng*	Wait a while
	zài	He/she's here
	bú zài zhèr	He/she's not here

At a restaurant

Basics

Q: *nǐmen jǐwèi?*	How many (of you)?
A: *wǒmen wǔ ge rén*	There are five of us
wǒmen liǎng ge rén	There are two of us
Q: *nǐmen chī shénme?*	What will you eat?
A: *wǒmen chī . . .*	We'll eat . . .
mǐfàn	Rice
miàntiáo	Noodles
mántou	Steamed rolls
jiǎozi	Dumplings
sānge cài yíge tāng	Three dishes, one soup
shí kuai qián de biāozhǔn	A meal to a ten *yuan* standard
qíng nǐ jièshao jǐge cài	Please suggest some dishes
Q: *nǐmen hē shénme?*	What will you drink?
A: *wǒmen hē . . .*	We'll drink . . .
píjiǔ	Beer
Lǎoshān shuǐ	Laoshan mineral water
qìshuǐ	Fizzy drink, soda-pop
kělè	Cola

Preferences

wǒ xǐhuan chī . . .	I like to eat . . .
wǒ bù néng chī . . .	I can't eat . . .
zhūròu	Pork
yú	Fish
là de	Spicy food
sù de	Vegetarian food
wèijīng	Monosodium glutamate

Endings

To get a waiter's attention, call *shīfu:*

suànzhàng	(We'll) settle the bill

Shopping

Q: *nǐ yào/mǎi shénme?*	What do you want/What are you buying?
A: *wǒ yào/mǎi*	I want/am buying . . .
zhèige	This one
nèige	That one
Q: *ní yǒu méi yǒu . . .?*	Do you have . . .?
dà yìdiǎn de	A bigger one
xiǎo yìdiǎn de	A smaller one
qù Běijīng de fēijīpiào	A plane ticket to Beijing
qù Shànghǎi de huǒchēpiào	A rail ticket to Shanghai

A: *yǒu/méi yǒu*	(We) have (some)/(We) don't have (any)
Q: *hái yǒu ma?*	Do you have any more?

Note: méi yǒu, 'we don't have it', and *méi yǒu le*, 'we don't have it any more', are two of the commonest expressions in the language.

Q: *duōshao qián?* How much?

Note: Sums of money are composed of *kuài 'yuan'*, *máo* '10 cents' and *fēn* 'cents'. Thus:

A: *sānshí kuài qián*	30 *yuan*
A: *sì kuài wǔ máo qī*	4.57 *yuan*

wǒ mǎi liùge/bāge	I'll buy six/eight
tài guì le	It's too expensive

Numbers

1 *yī*, 2 *èr*, 3 *sān*, 4 *sì*, 5 *wǔ*,
6 *liù*, 7 *qī*, 8 *bā*, 9 *jiǔ*, 10 *shí*,

11 *shí'yī*,	12 *shí'èr*,	13 *shísān* etc.
20 *èrshí*,	21 *èrshí'yī*,	22 *èrshí' èr* etc.
30 *sānshí*	40 *sìshí*	50 *wǔshí* etc.
100 *yì bǎi*	1,000 *yì qiān*	10,000 *yí wàn*

The number 34,567 is 3 ten-thousands, 4 thousands, 5 hundreds, six tens and 7 units, thus: *sān wàn sì qiān wú bǎi liùshí qī*.

Note: for the number two, *èr* is used in counting and making compound numbers; if you just want to talk about two of something, use *liǎng*. Thus *liǎng ge rén*, 'two people', but *èrshi'èr ge rén*, 'twenty-two people'.

Body language

Smiling/laughter: is used to indicate embarrassment and nervousness as well as amusement or happiness

Pointing: it is rude to point at others. To indicate yourself, point to your nose

Nodding: is used for greeting, thanking and deference as well as agreement

Refusing: is done with the palm facing out and waved in front of the body

Useful addresses

Chinese embassies and consulates

Australia Embassy: 14, Federal Highway, Watson, Canberra, ACT 2602. Tel: 412448

Canada Embassy: 415 St Andrew St., Ottawa, Ontario K1N 5H3. Tel: (613) 234-2706
Consulate-General: 240 St George Street, Toronto, Ontario M5R 2P4. Tel: (416) 964-7260
Consulate-General: 3380 Granville Street, Vancouver, BC, V6H 3K3. Tel: (604) 736-3910, 736-4021

New Zealand Embassy: 2–6 Glenmore Street, Wellington. Tel: 721383

UK Embassy: 31 Portland Place, London W1N 3AG. Tel: (071) 636-5637

USA Embassy: 2300 Connecticut Avenue NW, Washington, DC 20008. Tel: (202) 328-2520. Telex: 440038 PRC U1
Consulate-General: 3417 Montrose Blvd, Houston, Texas 77052. Tel: (713) 524-4064, 524-4311
Consulate-General: 520 12th Avenue, New York, NY 10036. Tel: (212) 330-7428
Consulate-General: 1450 Laguna St., San Francisco, California 94115. Tel: (415) 563-4857, 563-4858
Consulate-General: 104 S. Michigan Ave, Suite 120, Chicago, Illinois 60603
Consulate-General: 501 Shatto Place, Suite 300, Los Angeles, California 90020. Tel: (213) 380-3105

Foreign embassies and consulates in China

Australia Embassy: 15 Dongzhimenwai Street, Sanlitun, Beijing. Tel: 52-2331
Consulate-General: 17 Fuxing Road West, Shanghai. Tel: 33-4604

Canada Embassy: 10 Sanlitun Road, Sanlitun North, Beijing. Tel: 52-1475

Consulate-General: 4th Floor, Union Building, 100 Yan'an Road East, Shanghai. Tel: 20-2822

New Zealand
Embassy: 1 Ritan Road East, Jianguomenwai, Beijing. Tel: 52-2731

UK
Embassy: 11 Guanghua Road, Jianguomenwai, Beijing. Tel: 52-1961
Consulate-General: 244 Yongfu Road, Shanghai. Tel: 37-4569. Telex: 33140

USA
Embassy: 3 Xiushui Street North, Jianguomenwai, Beijing. Tel: 532-3831
Consulate-General: Jinjiang Hotel, 180 Renmin Road, Chengdu, Sichuan. Tel: 28-24481
Consulate-General: Dongfang Hotel, Guangzhou. Tel: 669-900
Consulate-General: 1469 Huaihai Road Central, Shanghai. Tel: 33-6880
Consulate-General: Sanjing St, Heping District, Shenyang, Liaoning. Tel: 29-0038

Friendship organizations

Australia
Australia–China Society, 228 Gertrude Street, Fitzroy, Victoria

Canada
Federation of Canada–China Friendship Associations, 2420 Douglas Street, Victoria, BC, V8T 4L7

New Zealand
New Zealand–China Friendship Society, 22 Swanson Street, Auckland

UK
Society for Anglo-Chinese Understanding, 16 Portland Street, Cheltenham, Gloucester GL52 2PB

USA
US–China Peoples Friendship Association, 2025 Eye Street NW, Suite 715, Washington DC 20006

Trade councils

Canada
Canada–China Trade Council, 199 Bay Street, Suite 805, Toronto, Ontario K5J 1L4. Tel: (416) 364-8231

UK
Sino-British Trade Council, Abford House, Wilton Road, London SW1. Tel: (071) 828-5176

USA
National Council for US–China Trade, 1050 17th Street NW, Suite 350, Washington, DC 20036. Tel: (202) 828-8300

Travel

CITS Head Office: 6 Chang'an Avenue East, Beijing. Tel: 55-1031. Cable: Luxingshe Beijing. Telex: 22350 CITSH CN

Hong Kong: 601/605/606, 6th Floor, Tower II, South Sea Centre, Tsimshatsui East, Kowloon. Tel: 3-7215317. Cable 2320 Hong Kong. Telex: 38449 CITC HX

UK: 4 Glenworth Street, London NW1. Tel: (071) 935-9427

USA: 60E, 42nd Street, Suite 465, New York, NY 10065. Tel: (212) 867-0271

Further reading

History

Joan Lebold Cohen and Jerome Alan Cohen, *China Today and Her Ancient Treasures*. New York: Abrams, 1986.
Pictorial history of China.

Pan Ling, *In Search of Old Shanghai*. Hong Kong: Joint Publishing, 1982.
The most readable history of China's most exciting city.

Richard J. Smith, *China's Cultural Heritage: The Ch'ing Dynasty 1644–1912*. Boulder, Colorado: Westview Press, 1983.
Introduction to all aspects of the Chinese tradition.

Jonathon D. Spence, *The Gate of Heavenly Peace: The Chinese and Their Revolution 1895–1980*. New York: Viking, 1981.
History of twentieth century China told through the biographies of leading political and cultural figures.

Jonathon D. Spence, *To Change China: Western Advisers in China 1620–1960*. Harmondsworth: Penguin, 1980.
The adventures of foreign advisers from Jesuits to Soviets.

Events of June 1989

Han Minzhu, *Cries for Democracy*. Princeton, New Jersey: Princeton University Press, 1990.
Writings and speeches from the democracy movement.

Liu Binyan, *Tell the World*. New York: Pantheon, 1990.
Description of the events of June 1989, and analysis of their origins in Chinese society.

Scott Simmie and Bob Nixon, *Tiananmen Square*. Toronto: Douglas and McIntyre, 1989.
The best of several Western accounts.

Society

Liang Heng and Judith Shapiro, *Son of the Revolution*. New York: Random House, 1983.
Autobiography of Liang Heng, who came of age in Cultural Revolution China and is now a leader of the movement in America for Chinese democracy.

Orville Schell, *To Get Rich is Glorious: China in the 1980s*. New York: Mentor, 1986.
About the changes in Chinese society and the author's culture-shocked reaction to them.

Orville Schell, *Discos and Democracy*. New York: Pantheon, 1988.
More of the same.

Zhang Xinxin and Sang Ye, *Chinese Lives*, translated by W. H. F. Jenner and Delia Davin. New York: Random House, 1988.
Enlightening oral history of contemporary China.

Guidebooks

China Guides Series: titles include *All China*; *Peking (Beijing)*; *Shanghai*; *Guilin; Canton (Guangzhou) and Guangdong; Hangzhou*; *Nanjing, Suzhou and Wuxi*; *Xi'an*; *Yunnan*; *Hong Kong*. Hong Kong: China Guides Series Ltd.
Handy and regularly updated series, with details of attractions, restaurants and stores.

Frederic Kaplan, Julian M. Sobin and Arne de Keizer, *The China Guidebook*. Boston: Houghton Mifflin, 1988.

Frances Wood, *China*. London: Blue Guides, 1990.
These are probably the best of the one-volume China guides currently available. The competition includes *Fielding's Guide* and *Fodor's Guide*.

Alan Samagalski and Michael Buckley, *China: A Travel Survival Kit*. South Yarra, Australia: 1988.

Catharine Sanders, Chris Stewart and Rhonda Evans, *The Rough Guide to China*. London: Routledge and Kegan Paul, 1987.
These two are detailed guides designed for the solo traveller, with good advice on getting around cheaply. Both tend to be disdainful of those who travel any other way; the *Survival Kit* also has a regrettably superior attitude to the Chinese.

Living in China

The Foreign Experts' Handbook. Beijing: New World Press, 1988.
Guide to living and working in China prepared by the State Bureau of Foreign Experts.

William Goede, *Love in Beijing and Other Stories*. Dunvegan, Ontario: Cormorant Books, 1988.
Stories about 'expert' life in Beijing.

Mark Salzman, *Iron and Silk*. New York: Random House, 1986.
Humorous and insightful memoirs of a new American China-hand as teacher and martial-arts student in China.

Business

Almanac of China's Foreign Economic Relations and Trade. Hong Kong: Joint Publishing, published annually.
Released by MOFERT, contains policy statements, texts of laws and regulations, economic statistics and other very useful information.

Arne de Keizer, *The China Business Handbook*. Weston, Connecticut: Asia Business Communications, 1986.
Practical advice derived from experience of China business.

Robert Delfs, Thomas D. Gorman and Owen D. Nee, Jr, *China*. London: Euromoney, 1986.
Contains essays on politics, trade and law, with case histories.

Jim Mann, *Beijing Jeep: The Short Unhappy Romance of American Business in China*. New York: Simon and Schuster, 1989.
A case study of a highly-publicized Joint Venture.

Shopping

Roberta Stalberg, *Shopping in China: Arts, Crafts and the Unusual*. San Francisco: China Books, 1986.
Useful listings of shops and products.

Food

Chinese Cooking. Beijing: Zhaohua, 1983.
General cookbook available in China.

Robert Delfs, *The Good Food of Szechwan*. New York: Kodansha/Harper and Row, 1979.
Authentic cooking made easy; the authors' favorite cookbook.

Kenneth Lo, *Chinese Regional Cooking*. New York: Pantheon, 1979.
One of many excellent books by the dean of Chinese cookbook writers.

Language

John DeFrancis, *The Chinese Language: Fact and Fantasy*. Honolulu: University of Hawaii Press, 1986.
Scholarly but jolly debunking of myths about the language.

Phrase-books and text-books

Beth McKillop, *Travellers' Chinese*. London: Pan Books, 1990.
Useful pocket-size phrase-book.

Beverly Hong, *Situational Chinese*. Beijing: New World Press, 1983.
Combination phrase-book and textbook for those who already know some Chinese.

P.C.T'ung and David Pollard, *Colloquial Chinese*. London: Routledge, 1982.
A first-year university course in Chinese. (Tapes and Chinese text are available from the School of Oriental and African Studies at the University of London.)

English-Chinese dictionary

The Pocket English–Chinese (Pinyin) Dictionary. Shanghai: Commercial Press, 1983.
Good small dictionary with Chinese words given in characters and pinyin.

Translations of Chinese literature

Geremie Barmé and John Minford, *Seeds of Fire: Chinese Voices of Conscience*. New York: Hill and Wang, 1989.
Short extracts, with commentary, of some of the best writing of the 1980s.

Cyril Birch, *Anthology of Chinese Literature*. Harmondsworth: Penguin, 1967.
A varied collection of classical literature to the fourteenth century.

Cao Xueqin, *The Story of the Stone* (5 volumes), translated by David Hawkes (vols 1–3) and John Minford (vols 4 and 5). Harmondsworth: Penguin, 1986.
Splendid translation of China's great eighteenth century novel, also called *The Dream of the Red Chamber*.

Lao She, *Rickshaw*, translated by Jean M. James. Honolulu: University of Hawaii Press, 1986.
The best novel of the republican period, about a rickshaw-puller's inability to cope with the pressures of capitalism.

Zhang Xianliang, *Half of Man is Woman*, translated by Martha Avery. Harmondsworth: Viking, 1988.
A novel about prison-camps and sexuality which shocked many Chinese readers when it appeared in 1985.

Chinese women

Emily Honig and Gail Herschatter, *Personal Voices: Chinese Women in the 1980s*. Stanford: Stanford University Press, 1988.
Includes essays and translations dealing with work, sexuality, family, violence, etc.

Village China

Pat Howard, *Breaking the Iron Rice-bowl: Prospects for Socialism in China's Countryside*. Armonk, New York: M.E. Sharpe, 1988.
Review of the changes in rural China from a Western socialist perspective.

Stephen W. Mosher, *Broken Earth: The Rural Chinese*. New York: The Free Press, 1983.
Damning eye-witness account of village life in the early 1980s in Guangdong province.

Glossary

Acronyms	CAAC	Civil Aviation Administration of China
	CITS	China International Travel Service
	CP	Communist Party
	FEC	Foreign Exchange Certificate (Chinese currency for foreigners)
	JV	Joint Venture (company formed by Chinese and foreign investors)
	PSB	Public Security Bureau (Police)
	RMB	*Renminbi* (Standard Chinese currency)
	SEZ	Special Economic Zone
Chinese terms	*biaozhun*	Standard rate (for meals)
	gongfei	Publicly funded (student on exchange programme)
	guanxi	Connections, and the system for using them
	zifei	Privately funded (student in China at his or her own expense)
English words with different meanings in China	cadre	Official
	expert	Foreigner working for a Chinese organization, for example as a teacher or technical adviser
	unit	Place of employment or study; organization responsible for you

Index